Patrick J. **Nov**

A Student's Introduction to
Political Analysis

Kendall Hunt
publishing company

Kendall Hunt
publishing company

www.kendallhunt.com
Send all inquiries to:
4050 Westmark Drive
Dubuque, IA 52004-1840

Copyright © 2018 by Kendall Hunt Publishing Company

ISBN 978-1-5249-5143-6

Published in the United States of America

DEDICATION

To my wife, Theresa Beebe Novotny

TABLE OF CONTENTS

INTRODUCTION

I have a lifetime of family, friends, colleagues, students, and especially teachers to thank for inspiring me to write *A Student's Introduction to Political Analysis*. I can say with no doubt whatsoever that this is the most difficult part of this book to write. I have so many people to thank for their inspiration and their encouragement that shaped this book. I know I cannot possibly begin to adequately thank enough the people I will mention in the next several pages, and I know for every person I mention in the coming pages, there will be those I leave out who are deserving of recognition. I regret omission of the names of those who I know I will leave out through no intention on my part except the imperfection of recollection.

When I began writing this book in December 2016, I had just finished teaching my first section of a course I had advocated that we to create for our students in the Department of Political Science and International Studies at Georgia Southern University, POLS 2130 Introduction to Political Analysis. I was lucky to have a group of enthusiastic students in my first section of POLS 2130, and I tried out new ideas with them throughout the Semester to share my enthusiasm and my excitement of reading, research, and writing. As the Fall 2016 Semester came to a close, I was struck by the possibility of writing a book that would capture some of the ideas that I had taught in that Semester. I came up with working titles for several of the tentative chapters for the book, and then spent several days at the end of the Fall 2016 Semester with these chapter titles projected as slides to the students in the class to allow them to brainstorm with me on the relevant subjects and topics from our Semester's class that would go into the appropriate chapters.

When I started outlining ideas for the book in December 2016, I did so almost entirely on my phone, typing away with my thumbs on a Google Doc as I traveled across the country with my wife for the holidays visiting our families. I spent hours of time that I would have read the articles or books I typically bring with me on trips instead tapping away on my phone writing on the subjects for the respective chapters I had outlined with my POLS 2130 students in November. In January and February, my ideas did not slow down, and by March, almost immediately upon finishing a six-chapter book I had been writing on the history of political parties in American politics, I started to write the earliest drafts of what would become the first chapter of this book.

As I discuss in Chapter 3, I spent several weeks in March and April trying to find just the right subject and starting point for this book's first chapter. I went through several different drafts of openings for the first chapter that just did not work for me and left me feeling like I might not ever be able to get this project started, let alone finish it. I had a Semester's educational leave for the Fall 2017 Semester, and had visions of working on this project well into that Fall with possibly no end in sight if I couldn't get even the opening pages of the book's first chapter the way I wanted it to be.

It took weeks to finally settle on what is now the book's opening that you will read at the beginning of Chapter 1. Once I had the beginning of Chapter 1 where I liked it, the words in this book came remarkably easy and were the culmination of almost 30 years of thinking about the academic discipline of political science. Once I finished with Chapter 1, Chapters 2 through 6 came almost as quickly as I could write from many pages of notes I had typed on my phone through Google Docs. I spent some very enjoyable days in May 2017 reading about Ernest Hemingway, especially his employment as a young man as a reporter with *The Kansas City Star*, William Faulkner, and other writers as well as thinking about people like former Black Flag lead singer Henry Rollins and others who I think have so much to say to students about the importance of travel and seeing the world firsthand and experiencing the places and meeting the people that we write about in political science or in any other field. I wrote this book with an enjoyment and an enthusiasm that had so much to do with both the students who had inspired me in the Fall 2016 Semester's POLS 2130 and the family and friends whose encouragement made this book possible.

For the friendship and the encouragement that made this book possible, I can thank no one else more than my dear friends, Connie and Merle Clark. Connie and Merle have been such close friends for many years, and they are truly some of the kindest, most hardworking, fun-loving people I know. In the months of April and May of 2017, it was Connie and Merle whose conversations with me as I talked about the ideas I was working on in this book that made this book possible. I found myself visiting with Connie and Merle almost every afternoon after the writing sessions in my office. Their words of encouragement (not to mention the great timing of a large new tent and sitting area next their swimming pool and the celebratory cigar at the end of each chapter) kept me going in writing this book when I needed it the most. Connie, Merle, their children Austin, Emilee, and Sarah, their families, especially Connie's mother, Deborah Bland Cato, and Merle's mother, Bonnie Clark, Connie's sister, Wendy, her daughters Ayla and Tala and husband Jay, and so many other members of the Cato and Clark families all were such a wonderful source of friendship for me as I wrote this book. Connie and Merle were with me every step of the way when I began writing this book, and they were there celebrating with me in July 2017, along with my wife Theresa, as I finalized my arrangements with Kendall Hunt for this book's publication. I simply cannot thank Connie and Merle enough for their many years of friendship, encouragement, and most of all, their willingness to listen to me talk about my research and my writing. I will never forget texting them both as I wrote sentences in this book telling them, "this sentence is about you" or "I wrote this after we talked about this" or some such. I owe Connie and Merle more than I could ever put into words for their graciousness and generosity as my dear friends over the years and for giving me the encouragement when I needed it the most to finish this book.

I dedicate this book to my wife, Theresa Beebe Novotny, for her love and understanding and help with every part of this book. I wrote this book tapping with my thumbs and typing on my phone in Google Docs with Theresa almost always sitting next to me reading a book on her

Kindle or just spending time together with me, always understanding every time I reached for the phone to make some additional notes in Google Docs or every time I came in to our living room to share with her my latest idea for the book. Most of my books begin as conversations we have on the walks in the evening that Theresa and I take so many evenings for our exercise, and this book is no exception. In our many hours of walking and conversation in our quiet neighborhood in the evenings, we talked through almost every single idea in almost every single sentence of this book, ideas that are, as always, so much better because of Theresa's advice and suggestions along the way. I could not do what I do without Theresa, and I owe her everything for her patience, her understanding, and for allowing me to spend the long hours in the library or in my office while writing this book. We have shared so many travels and experiences together that are on its pages, and I look forward to spending many more years together with Theresa traveling and exploring the places like the many that helped inspire me in writing this book.

I owe special thanks to my wife's parents, Les and Wilma Beebe, for their love and support in the time we spend together visiting whenever we have the chance to see them. I treasure our visits to their home in Lynchburg, Virginia, and I always enjoy the time Theresa and I have there to spend with her mother and father and their friends. Lynchburg is a special place, and I always enjoy spending time there with her family whenever we can. Sadly, in April 2017, Theresa's grandmother, Carol Selby, passed away in Lynchburg. Her strength and spirit and smile always lifted me up every time we visited her, and I enjoyed visiting with Carol and spending time with her whenever we visited Lynchburg. I will miss Carol dearly, and her spirit and strength she shared with her granddaughter, Theresa, is a source of happiness and comfort in my life every day.

I have so many friends to thank for this book that it is almost an exercise in futility to begin listing them. I know even before I start writing this that I will inadvertently leave out friends, colleagues, former students, and so many others who have shaped the ideas in this book, but I would hope that my many friends know without being mentioned individually just how important each one of you are to the writing that I do in books like this. I want to thank some of the many friends who are a part of my weekly coffee groups that meet for good conversation and a cup or two of the coffee. I especially want to thank dear friends and coffee group conversationalists George Shriver, John Daily, Lane Van Tassell, Darin Van Tassell, Nick Henry, and others whose conversations over coffee kept me going in writing this book. Tony Barilla, Mark Welford, Michael Moore, Paul Rodell, and others have certainly been a big part of my weekly sessions as well at Statesboro's Sugar Magnolia Bakery, and I truly appreciate their listening to me talk about my writing of this book. Barry Turner, the owner of Sugar Magnolia Bakery, is a dear friend and I appreciate him always taking the time to visit with me whenever I come to the bakery and letting me enjoy endless refills of coffee as I sat many hours in Sugar Magnolia thinking about many of the ideas in the pages of this book. Phil Boyum is a friend who I have always turned to for advice in every one of my writing projects in the past 10 years or so, and he always is one of my favorite people to try out so many of the ideas that eventually make their way onto the pages of books like this one. I appreciate Phil always taking the time to let me talk through my ideas with him before they make it on to the page, and his years of friendship mean the world to me. Alison Lyall is always there with a friendly conversation or an e-mail or text message when I am writing, and I appreciate her friendship dearly. My friends with the Bulloch County Historical Society, especially Executive Director Virginia Anne Franklin Waters and her husband, Bill, President Joe McGlamery, and my fellow Executive Board members and others kept me on track as I wrote this book, and I thank Virginia Anne, Joe, and our Executive Board for giving me the chance to be a part of such a special group here in Statesboro, to keep alive the history and the stories of a town and a place that I love to call home.

Georgia Southern University faculty colleagues and students who helped along the way in writing this book are too numerous to mention here, but certainly Barry Balleck, Chair of the Department of Political Science and International Studies at Georgia Southern University, is first and foremost for his support and encouragement, especially to apply for an Educational Leave in the Fall 2017 to finish the preparation of the publication of this book. My friend and coauthor Darin Van H. Tassell is a special colleague whose friendship and words of encouragement have made a difference like no other colleague in my career. I would not have written this book without the encouragement and support of Darin as we worked on the second edition of our book, *Listening, Looking, Living*. I am so incredibly honored and humbled and proud to have known and worked with Darin since the first day I set foot on the Georgia Southern University campus back in August 1995, and our friendship and work together has been instrumental in everything I have done in those years since we first met back in 1995. Darin and Barry are colleagues and friends who together have sustained my work over the decades, and I simply cannot find words enough to thank them both for everything they have done.

Jared Yates Sexton graciously read an early draft of this book in the middle of his own work copyediting his book, *The People are Going to Rise Like the Waters Upon Your Shore: A Story of American Rage*. I am honored and privileged to work with a colleague of Jared's talent as a writer, and I have benefitted immensely from having the chance to work with him in our writing and our teaching at Georgia Southern University. Lindsay Gribble took on different tasks very early in my writing of this book, and I thank Lindsay so much for her help and assistance to get this project off the ground as well as her willingness to read drafts of several of the chapters of this book early on just as they were in their formative stage. I appreciate her keen insight, attention to detail, and her hard work at the early stages of this book to help with some of the assembling of materials that made their way into it. Students in my POLS 2130 Introduction to Political Analysis inspired this book, and two of the students from that class in the Fall 2016, Julianne Stewart and Jarvis Steele, went above and beyond the call of duty in volunteering to read drafts of chapters almost as quickly as I wrote them in May 2017, and provide feedback to me that helped to shape and guide ideas in this book. Narayan Saviskas went out of his way as well to help with the early stages of this manuscript, and Narayan volunteered to read drafts of several chapters as well, making these chapters much stronger based upon his feedback and that of my other former students. To Julianne, Jarvis, Narayan, and the many students I have been honored and humbled to teach in my years at Georgia Southern University, I owe you, my students at Georgia Southern University, everything for all you have done to inspire me and help me think through and think about so many of the ideas in this book.

I owe a special thanks to David and Fayebeth Ball for the hospitality in a visit to their family's property on Georgia's Cumberland Island as I completed this book. David and Fayebeth are some of the kindest, most generous and gracious people I have had the pleasure to meet since I moved to Georgia back in 1995, and I was fortunate to have a chance to visit their family property on Cumberland Island and take in the richness of the island's beaches, forests, and especially its history and its story as a part of Georgia's history. David did his best to help me find a particular location on the island that I had hoped might be photographed for use on the cover of this book, but it proved to be too difficult for us to manage on that particular visit, something that anyone familiar with Cumberland Island's remoteness and ruggedness of terrain will appreciate. I am so grateful and so moved by the generosity and hospitality of David and Fayebeth in their invitation to visit Cumberland Island, and I promised David if we ever manage to photograph that particular location, it will certainly make the cover for a second or third edition of this book.

I would be remiss if I did not express my heartfelt thanks and appreciation to Connor J. Schreck with Kendall Hunt Publishing Company. Connor has been a source of much-appreciated support from the very earliest stages of my writing this book. I am so grateful to Connor for his attentiveness and his encouragement and support in seeing this book through all the way from its inception to its publication. Connor's conversations on the telephone with me in June 2017 and after as I completed this book, and his work with me as the book moved into its copyediting and production phases is so greatly appreciated. I am grateful to have had the chance to work with Connor on this book, and it is thanks to him that this book was completed well ahead of my initial schedule. Connor's encouragement saw me through this project, and I owe him so much for his support and help at every stage of the process. Stefani L. Demoss and Lynne Rogers also were instrumental as part of the Kendall Hunt Publishing Company team who worked with me on this book, and I can't thank them enough. I want to express my thanks to everyone at Kendall Hunt Publishing for the work they do in bringing books like this in an accessible, affordable way to the hands of students in the classroom.

I finally want to express my heartfelt thanks to my parents, John Novotny and Margaret Novotny, for their love and support and encouragement of the lifetime of experiences and study that are represented here in the pages of this book. In September 2017, my father passed away quite unexpectedly. I spent so many difficult days in the weeks after his passing thinking not only of the sadness and sorrow my mother and I felt with his passing, but also the joy and the love that he and my mother shared with me my entire life. My father tirelessly supported every part of my education and my learning and my studies and my travel. My father was a source of inspiration for everything I did and still do in my research and my learning and my love of travel and reading and studying and writing. He spent many hours in his years of retirement reading and writing on his own book projects, correspondence, and the neighborhood newsletter at his computer looking out at the Mississippi River from our home. My father loved to write, and I loved sharing a passion for writing and for reading and for learning with my father. I am blessed in my life to have had parents who always understood the importance of travel and learning and studying and education. There was never a vacation or a trip that wasn't paid for, never a book that I couldn't buy as a child growing up, never a bill for tuition or an expense of some kind that my father and mother were not ready to help with a generosity and a support that I hope I share with the family and friends around me in my life today.

I miss my father since his passing, and I have spent many days with my mother working through the tears and the heartache we feel but also celebrating in our memories his love of us both and the warmth and generosity and kindness of his spirit. I am truly inspired by my mother, and her strength and spirit as she has held our family together as she always has and always will. I am truly blessed to have my father and my mother as role models and inspirations and as a source of unwavering support in everything I have done in my life. I hope that my father and my mother would be familiar with the ideas and thinking on every page of this book. I only could have written this book with their love and support and encouragement and their life of instilling in me the importance of reading and of traveling and of learning and education. I love my family for their caring, their generosity, their kindness, and most of all their love of learning and knowledge and education. I owe my mother and father everything, and I know in my heart without their love and support, not a single word of this book would have ever been possible.

Patrick J. Novotny is a Professor in the Department of Political Science and International Studies at Georgia Southern University, where he began teaching in the Fall of 1995. Publishing his early work on the environmental justice movement and the environmental activism of low-income and working-class whites, African-Americans, Latinos, and others, Novotny's work increasingly focused on the study of American political life and the dynamics of institutions as shaped by external forces, not only in political movements, but also in the realm of the arts, literature, music, and most especially the press. His book, *The Press in American Politics, 1787–2012* (Praeger), is a part of his longstanding writing on the history and the contemporary dynamics of advertising and the Internet and World Wide Web in campaigning and elections in American politics. His work continues with his recent completion of a book-length manuscript on the history of political parties in American politics, a book which explores many themes including the impact of the press on America's political parties from the newspapers of the 1780s through the radio and television broadcasting of the 20th century and the digital communications and media of the Internet and the World Wide Web today. Novotny's work also includes his research on the history and dynamics of the 20th century politics and political change in Georgia, the early history of commercial television broadcasting in the state, and especially the early history of the 20th century civil rights movement in Georgia, research published in several works, including essays in *The Georgia Historical Quarterly* and in his 2007 book, *This Georgia Rising: Education, Civil Rights, And The Politics Of Change In Georgia In The 1940s* (Mercer University Press). Novotny's co-authored book, *Listening, Looking, Living: Qualitative Research, the Study of Politics, and Understanding the World in Which We Live* (Kendall Hunt), is in its 2nd edition. With the completion of *A Student's Introduction to Political Analysis* (Kendall Hunt), Novotny is now writing a book-length manuscript on the history of music in American political life. Novotny was recognized for commitment to his students in the classroom as the recipient of Georgia Southern University's 2004–2005 Wells-Warren Professor of the Year award.

CHAPTER 1

Why Who Gets What, When, How?

Harold Lasswell said it all about politics, and he said it simply: who gets what, when, how. It seems about right, and it seems to all be right there. It's straightforward. It's hard to see what is left out. It's easy to explain. It's even easier to remember. It sums it up. It's the starting point for Chapters 1 and 2 of almost every textbook used in most Introduction to American Government courses.[1] Who could argue with it? Why would you even want to? What could possibly be missing? What else needs to be said?

Who gets what, when, how. It's easy to see its obvious appeal. It's reliable, and it's relatable to almost anything and everything. Nothing is out-of-place in those five-words-and-two-commas, and it's not going to lead you astray or steer you wrong. Nothing's going to get past it as a simple, straightforward definition of politics. Not only is it easy to explain, but it's also going to explain almost everything. No need for finer points or nuance. There's nothing that's going to be left out. Or so it would seem.

But if we look at it a bit more closely and if we think about it for just a bit longer, it may not be enough to help us answer most of our questions when it comes to thinking about the dynamics and forces at work in politics. We might start by asking ourselves a simple question. Why isn't there a <u>why</u> in who gets, what, when, how? Isn't it important for us to think about intent and motive when we try to understand politics? Simply put: shouldn't we think about <u>why</u> it is that people do what they do? Aren't their interests, their motives, their purposes, their rationales something we need to consider when we study politics? Isn't the way that they explain and put into their own words what they do in politics something that we always need to study when we study politics?

Why aren't we asking <u>why</u> people think the way they do when it comes to politics? Why aren't we considering how it is that people form the beliefs and ideas that motivate them when it comes to

---

[1] Harold Lasswell's, *Politics: Who Gets What, When, How*, 1st ed. (New York: McGraw Hill Book Company, 1936) and its paperback (Meridian Books, 1958) is far from the kinds of books most students today would pick up on their own if not assigned or required to read to understand and think about the forces at work in politics. Lasswell's book does not, in my opinion, stand as an especially clear or concise explanation of its title's promise. With few passages that stand particularly well on their own decades later, *Politics: Who Gets, What, When, How* is a book more likely to be cited and spoken of in passing than one assigned and read (or reread) by those who write of it today.

politics? Can't we miss a good deal if we don't understand <u>why</u> it is that people think about politics in the ways that they do? If incomplete information or a lack of knowledge is sometimes a part of why people act or think the way they do when it comes to politics, shouldn't we look at this? Wouldn't answers to most our questions tell us more if we look at the underlying motives and sometimes the misinformation that lead us to think and to act and to react in the ways that we do in politics?

The only way to understand why something happens in politics is knowing why people do what they do, and it means that we need to understand the intentions, the motivations, and the purposes that influence them. When we ask <u>why</u>, we can understand how impervious to change so many assumptions and beliefs are for so many people. It lets us consider the dispositions that sometimes may make it impossible for people to look at an issue or political figure with anything other than their already-formed opinions, making rational calculations more the exception than the rule when it comes to so many of the forces at play in political life. The hatreds and hard-feelings, the remembrances and the misremembrances, and the fears and hopes for the future, these all can more clearly be brought into focus when we ask why.

Why is it that the present tense (gets) is front and center in who gets what, when, how? Why is it so important emphasize who <u>gets</u> what, when, how <u>now</u>? Don't we want the insight that comes with looking at more than just the present? Isn't it only reasonable for us to also know what has come before? Shouldn't we know what decisions have been made before now and who has made these decisions (as well as who has been left out of making them) in the past? Isn't it useful for us to know where things stand today by knowing as much as we can about what has happened prior to now?

Figure 1.1

© Orhan Cam/Shutterstock.com

Nothing happens that isn't shaped by the past, so bringing in the past (who has gotten what, when how before <u>now</u>) is a way of giving us a better understanding of the events that have brought us to this point. The past is the present, and reminding ourselves to always take the time and do the work to ask who has done what before now is how we can connect with and to reflect on our Faulknerian past-is-never-dead. The study of politics is often about paying attention to decisions that have already been made and things already said and done. Who has gotten what in the <u>past</u> is often the only way we might ever have any insight into who gets what, when, how now.

And thinking along these lines, why isn't there also a <u>where</u> somewhere in there? Shouldn't we know more about where all of this is happening? Isn't it obvious that location is always a part of what we should be looking at and studying when we study politics? Everything happens somewhere, and asking <u>where</u> it is and how it matters can be a way for us to learn much more

Figure 1.2

© DL Dickson/Shutterstock.com

than just a location. It should be our practice in political science to connect ourselves with the places that always have a place in our politics. A few simple words—why or where—can be all the difference in understanding in a more well-thought way who gets what, when, and how.

I begin this book with Chapter 2 on reading, because I think reading in a mindful, practiced way is the foundation of everything else we do as researchers and writers. I think reading is unfortunately too often seen as a means-to-an-end, as something that needs to be done at the beginning of our research but not as something that is a continuous part of the research and the writing that we do as students of politics. I think reading is much too important to be compartmentalized as something we do just at the beginning of our research when we assemble our literature views.

I feel reading is the most important thing that we do as researchers and as writers, and that it is so important that I believe we need to take the time to think clearly about what it is that we read and how it is that we read. It is something we need to do constantly, and it is our way of constantly enlivening and enriching our writing with the events and the stories that engage and excite our readers. It is something that we need to be more aware of at every step in our work, not just something that we do at the beginning of our writing when we are assembling research for a bibliography or a literature review.

Figure 1.3

© A and N Photography/Shutterstock.com

It is important that we look carefully in everything that we read for every possible connection and every unexpected lead that, in turn, takes us to still more connections and leads to still more writings we would never find otherwise unless we keep turning the pages. We read widely in the hope that we will find that article by the author we have never heard of before or that overlooked article we have never run across before now by the author whose works we thought we knew well. It is always about widening our frame of reference and expanding our focus. It is also about reading widely enough that we find the book here or the article there that we have never heard of before in the out-of-the-way; perhaps out-of-print places that sometimes yield the most insightful work. It is how we discover those writings that truly clarify and connect with the topics we are studying, even if we sometimes need to dig into the endnotes, footnotes, or bibliographies to find them.

The more widely-read we are, the more likely it is that our own writing will be enlivened with the detailed descriptiveness that too often lacks in so much of the work done in our field. The more well-read we are, the more likely it is we find the authors whose attention to detail and whose ability to bring words to life on their pages will inspire and instill in us the confidence to do the same when we write on our own. We read constantly and we look for as many details and insights as possible to enrich every sentence, paragraph, and page of our own writing.

Thinking about writing is the subject of Chapter 3 of this book as I turn from the work of reading to the commitment and the discipline that is essential in our writing. Writing is the most difficult and sometimes the most frustrating part of the research we do in our work as political scientists. When we read, our imagination wanders and our eyes sweep across pages looking for just the right insight, just the right example or instance of what we are studying or researching. When we write, the words we have read stare us back, inert, static, and waiting for us to bring them to life and spring them from our thoughts on to the page with the energy of our words.

Figure 1.4

© George Rudy/Shutterstock.com

I believe that there are no short-cuts when it comes to finding our voice and forming our confidence as a writer. Finding the expressive, self-confident, and unique voice we aspire to as writers is something that comes with time, and it is something that only comes with the work of reading and rereading, and considering and to reconsidering every sentence we write. It is all about the time you are willing to put in, and it is all about the time that you give to your words, poised and waiting for them to leap out through your fingertips.

The more willing that you are to work long hours at your writing, sometimes drumming your fingertips over the keyboard or tapping your pencil or pen on the page waiting for the words to come, the more likely that you will gain the confidence and the flow and the style of a successful writer. I believe that it is in these hours of staring at our sentences and paragraphs and pages where we find our own voice in our words. I think it is in the commitment to read and to reread the work that we write, where we find our own confidence as writers. I know in my own experience that there are few if any times when I cannot eventually write my way

Figure 1.5

© LightField Studios/Shutterstock.com

to the succinctness that I am seeking as a writer, if I only stick with it and give it the time that it takes to sometimes sort through and work through the words on the page. This takes hours of sometimes struggling with a page or two of writing, or even a paragraph, staring at the paper in front of me or looking at the screen, trying out a different word here or there, deleting some words, maybe erasing a sentence or more to take another swing at it, and always waiting and working for that moment that almost always arrives when the paragraphs and pages and words fall into place and do the work I want them to do for my reader.

Thinking about the place of history and thinking about incorporating the firsthand experiences and observations that come from exploring and connecting with places is the work of Chapters 4 and 5 of this book. I will make the case in Chapter 4 for students of political science to also become more careful students of a historical perspective in their work. I will encourage us to always consider a recognition of the relevant historical background when writing on the questions we are studying in political science.

"To read history and to become aware of its ambiguities," David M. Ricci tells us in his must-read *The Tragedy of Political Science: Politics, Scholarship, and Democracy*, "is to be reminded constantly of the dangers of learning about politics from books and articles that overemphasize the worth of figures and models."[2] The study of politics is and should always be clearly and closely

---

[2] David M. Ricci, *The Tragedy of Political Science: Politics, Scholarship, and Democracy* (New Haven: Yale University Press, 1984), 312.

intertwined with the study of history. Works of biography, writings that delve into the historical backgrounds of our institutions we study, and works that bring our attention to the changes and shifts in issues over time should never be far from the reading and the work of students of politics.

I think the insight that comes with working with historical documents and with primary sources whenever possible is far too important to simply be assumed when we think about the reading and the writing that we do in the study of political science. Instead of quoting a scholarly work that quotes a figure or person in the past, whenever possible I believe it is important for us to take the time to come as close as we can to finding these words in their original sources. If a book you are using has been published in multiple editions, it pays to take the time to look at the ideas of the author in their earliest editions.[3] It can give us sometimes important insight into the changes made by authors as they wrestle with their own ideas and thoughts over time. If you are telling the story of a specific event or moment in time, take the time to look at whatever newspapers or other documents or writings of the time you can get your hands on. Make the time to learn more about the lives of those whose influence we write about and whose leadership is a part of institutions we study.

"A page of history is worth a volume of logic," Justice Oliver Wendell Holmes, Jr. tells us in May 1921s <u>New York Trust Company</u>.[4] History, well-told, enlightens. It takes the long view. It expands our point of view in ways few other things can do. It is the wider view of

Figure 1.6

© Neveshkin Nikolay/Shutterstock.com

---

[3] In writing Chapter 3, I took the time to do something that I had not done in the years of my reading what I regard as the most important book I know on writing, William Strunk, Jr. and E. B. White's *The Elements of Style*. I purchased a somewhat tattered copy of a 1st edition of *The Elements of Style* to have as a part of my collection of works on writing, and to read as I thought about how to incorporate some of its well-known advice for generations of its readers into Chapter 3. I took the time to also read for the first time the famous article that appeared in July 1957 in the pages of *The New Yorker*, where White explored the ideas of the late William Strunk, Jr. that went into April 1959s 1st edition of this book. E. B. White, "Letter from the East," *The New Yorker* 33, no. 23 (July 27, 1957): 35–45.

[4] *New York Trust Company et al., as Executors of Purdy v. Eisner*, Error to the District Court of the United States for the Southern District of New York, No. 286, Argued April 25, 26, 1921, Decided May 16, 1921. *United States Reports, Volume 256, Cases Adjudged in the Supreme Court at October Term, 1920, from April 11, 1921 to June 6, 1921*. The Banks Law Publishing Company, 1922, 349.

history that compliments the close-up view of firsthand observation, observations that I will explore in Chapter 5. In everything we research and write on in our study of politics, the historical insights of tracing these ideas and institutions and issues back to their beginnings enlightens and enriches our readers.

I will use Chapter 5 to explore the use of firsthand observation and experiences to enrich our work and our writing. I feel that students in their studies of political science are best served when they are encouraged to take the wider view, to appreciate that politics is something so impacted and immersed in the culture and in the history surrounding it that students can only grasp it by seeing it firsthand and by taking the time to connect with specific places where they can watch it and form their own impressions. Politics is the stuff of culture, and culture is the stuff of how we live our lives and the way we learn our beliefs and our values and our ways of looking at the world. I know of no better way to study this than to see it ourselves, up close, firsthand. Distance is not the determinant of the insights gained in travel and in connecting with a place where we can study politics in its intersections with other parts of culture, history, and all aspects of life. Taking the time even if only to travel across town is every bit as meaningful to our insights as traveling halfway around the world.

I hope this book encourages each of us to think of the research we do in political science in the broadest terms possible. My hope is that the skills discussed in this book on reading, on writing, on incorporating a historical perspective, and the importance of firsthand observation connecting us with the places and the people who live there will together form the basis for a more creative, engaged, and inclusive approach to the study of politics, one that is engaged as much as possible with life in its richness and its complexity.

When we think about people and their many beliefs, ideas, perspectives, and points of view that they bring to politics, we can appreciate just how complicated the study of politics truly is. When we look at the past in the study of politics, we are again reminded how complicated and richly rewarding it can be not to just content ourselves with studying politics in the moment, but to step back from the present-tense and widen our thinking and our viewpoint to see what has happened in the past to bring us to where we are today. When we connect our work with the immediacy of place, it is a powerful connection and grounding for us as students of politics. People, past, place: these together tell us the story of politics in its complexity and in its connections to the events, the issues, and institutions we need to study.

I hope to encourage students in Chapter 6 to always make their work relevant and connected to the places where they live. Its title, "All Political Science is Local," is homage to the late House Speaker Tip O'Neill.[5] It pays for political scientists to have a street-level, world-wise familiarity with the places closest to home. I hope that we can take in as much information from as many sources as we can without limiting them to a few scholarly journals or well-footnoted sources. Sometimes, the most insight might come from the most unlikely sources. Sometimes, too, the most insight is found in listening to the voices not found in the pages of our journals or our peer-reviewed publications. It is important to connect to the stories

---

[5] Tip O'Neill, *Man of the House: The Life and Political Memoirs of Speaker Tip O'Neill* (New York: Random House, 1987), 6–26.

close to home that are not written down anywhere, stories more than likely never to be published in the pages of our journals or put to paper in our peer reviewed works.

As a political scientist who has taught for my career with an eye to expanding and widening the perspectives and the viewpoints of politics as widely as possible, I always make a point to urge my students to think of politics as something far too important and far too far-reaching to define in a single-sentence. Single-sentence definitions limit us too much for something as complicated as politics. No one-sentence definition is ever going to cut it. One-size-fits-all definitions rarely do us any favors in almost anything we study, and politics is something so complicated, that to define it in a sentence is always a disservice.

Figure 1.7
© VGstockstudio/Shutterstock.com

"You campaign in poetry," the late Mario Cuomo, Governor of New York, liked to say. "You govern in prose."[6] I share this with my students and weave it into lectures in my classes as a way of expressing the complicated, back-and-forth of politics as I see it. Cuomo's words speak to the compromise and deal making I believe is so much a part of governing. Concession is the constant. Coming up short is par-for-the-course. I give my students the best advice I think I can give, that feel-you-way-along, find-your-way-along, give-and-take is the given of our political institutions and our political ideas. Keeping all options on the table is often the only option for those in elective office in the prose of governing.

Where lawmakers well versed in the art of governing know well the adaptations and adjustments of their work, I feel that the student of

Figure 1.8   Mario Cuomo
© Juliet Kaye/Shutterstock.com

---

[6] Fred Barnes, "Is He the Last Liberal or a Lost Liberal? Meet Mario the Moderate," *The New Republic Monday*, April 8, 1985, 18.

political science is well-advantaged to the extent that they approach their own studies in an adaptable, inclusive, and open-minded way. Flexible, genuinely open-ended thinking about politics is my preference in the classroom, and give-and-take is my preference in the way I talk about and teach about and write about research. The nature of politics is that you take a point of view and you defend it, but also that you iron out your differences and find ways to compromise in the interest of either self-survival or in the pursuit of a larger, or a later, victory. I think the same thing can be just as easily be said about the flexible, open-ended thinking we need in the research in political science. Successful political scientists don't go in only looking for X, and ignore Y if they happen upon it, but instead political scientists who truly want to gain the greatest possible insight will look at everything, listen to everyone, go everywhere, make every adjustment and modification that is needed, and take from all this the clearest, most straightforward understanding we can. Keeping things flexible and loose in every step of our work is the only way we can ever hope to fully grasp the many different forces that frame our politics.

"Do as I say, not as I do" is a problem that I see with so many of the works and writings that teach our students about research in political science.[7] I see in Phillips Shively's *The Craft of Political Research* some of this limitation in such books for our students, yet in at least one part of Shively's book, I also take some comfort for his acknowledgement of this. I generally find *The Craft of Political Research* to be a disappointing volume when it comes to instilling the wider perspectives that I think students need when they begin their work to explore the study of politics and find their own style as researchers and voices as writers. *The Craft of Political Research*, now in its tenth edition, takes the reader through some of the steps of research in a relatively straightforward way. I say relatively, because for most readers, I am sure that Shively's work falls short of holding their interest unless they have a more specific commitment and a determination to learn some of the specific techniques put forth in his book. Despite its promising title, it is not especially accessible to readers not already well-versed in some of the more specialized research that is the bulk of its chapters. Shively veers almost immediately into a chapter-by-chapter analysis of statistical modeling and mathematical analysis that is not especially helpful for those hoping to have a wider introduction to the range of work done in the field.

---

[7] One of my favorite faculty back in my days a doctoral student at the University of Wisconsin-Madison, Chuck Jones, then on the faculty in Madison and an erudite scholar of American institutions, explores this in a must-read article, with the apt title, "Doing Before Knowing." In it, Jones assures his political science colleagues that while there is much room for scientific, systematic work in the field, too often we tend to overlook the importance of creativity, of insight in our interpretations. Urging us to push aside our interviews, our coding categories and classifications, and whatever other material we are analyzing to engage in what he calls contemplative reflection, Jones gets it right in thinking about the limits of what we can do in our field. Likewise, Jones also tweaks his colleagues when it comes to the teaching of research itself. "Writing about research methods," Jones says, "always makes them sound more rational and systematic than they ever are in fact." It is so often, he says, "anything but a tidy and confident procedure." More often, it is "a lengthy and none-too-systematic process" where creative and imaginative thought, "shuffling and prodding," even some old-fashioned trial-and-error are among those procedures that should be considered in the classroom. "We are still," Jones finishes, "very much a 'do as I say, not as I do' discipline when it comes to research methods." Charles O. Jones, "Doing Before Knowing: Concept Development in Political Research." *The American Journal of Political Science* 18, no. 1 (February 1974): 227.

But in Shively's opening pages, there is a pull-back-the-curtain moment where he earns my appreciation for telling us in no uncertain terms that the template taught to students is not necessarily the way many of their faculty themselves do their own work. It is in Shively's admission of the disconnect between so many of the fixed frameworks taught in so many classes and the much more flexible way that we as scholars undertake our own research. Shively earns my thanks for telling his readers that when it comes to research, the rigid formats taught are not necessarily those researchers adhere to when it comes to their own work. In pulling back the curtain to reveal that research is often done in a far looser and more iterative way than most faculty teach to their students, he is most certainly to be applauded.

We may assign rubrics or templates for our own students, but the reality is a much more reflective, relaxed, and resourceful style when it comes to our own work. Shively acknowledges this in the opening of his book, and I for one am grateful for his recognition of the point.

"One of the better-kept secrets in political science is that good political scientists generally do not draw up research designs before they start to work on a topic," Shively tells us in the opening pages of *The Craft of Political Research*.[8] "Nor do they usually 'frame hypotheses' in any formal sense before they start to work," Shively confides to the reader.[9] "Their procedure," Shively continues, now fully unencumbered of the façade still all too often foisted upon our students, "is less formal than the rules prescribe."[10] "They play with data, immerse themselves in what other people have written, argue with colleagues, and think."[11] Playing, immersing, arguing, and thinking. These are so important to the skills that we need as researchers of politics. "Most of us," Shively points out, "have better sense than to follow our own precepts."[12] Why Shively does relatively little in his book after saying this to

Figure 1.10

© wavebreakmedia/Shutterstock.com

expand and expound upon this idea is confusing to me every time that I thumb through one of the several different editions that I keep on the shelves in my office.

Politics is a bit of <u>everything</u> if it's anything. It's economics. It's history. It's geography. It's psychology. It's communication. It's science. It's technology and it's medicine. It's education. It's art. It's music. It's theater. It's poetry. It's prose. And it's all the places in between. Everything we study in political science is touched by culture, by history, by economics, by geography, by our traditions of faith, by our shared commitments, and disagreements of our beliefs and our ideas and our morals and values. Endlessly exhausting, fascinating in every way, there is nothing as complicated and infuriating and unpredictable in our lives as the politics that is always larger than elections won or lost, that is always greater than the candidates elected or defeated, that is always more than this or that bill enacted or blocked.

"Let us break with our formulas," Woodrow Wilson told us over a century ago when the study of government and politics grasped for the first time for the strictures of science.[13] Speaking at the seventh annual meeting of the American Political Science Association (APSA) in St. Louis in December 1910, Wilson urged his fellow political scientists to take a broad view of politics, to appreciate the "intricate life of men," as the Professor from Princeton put it, lives, in Wilson's words, "shot through" with tragedy and hope and all manner of "accidental elements." Empathy, sensitivity, and understanding: these are how we

---

[8] W. Phillips Shively, *The Craft of Political Research*, 10th ed. (New York: Routledge, 2017), 24.

[9] Ibid.

[10] Ibid.

[11] Ibid.

[12] Ibid.

[13] Woodrow Wilson, "The Law and the Facts." *The American Political Science Review* 5, no. 1 (February 1911): 10.

grasp and make sense of the human frailties of politics, Wilson said. "Nothing that forms or affects human life seems to me to be properly foreign to the student of politics," he explained.[14] "Politics is the very stuff of life." "Its relations are intensely human," not least of which is the "spiritual experience," "the visions of the mind," and "the aspirations of the spirit that are the pulse of life." Avoid classifications that are too fixed or systematic. "See the same facts from the points of view of many scores of men," Wilson advises. Yield to their passions and temperaments and "feel the pulse of their life" as you "put yourself in men's places," Wilson appeals to his fellow political scientists.

"Look at men everywhere first of all as at human beings struggling for existence, for a little comfort and ease of heart, for happiness amidst the things that bind and limit them."[15] Study people, Wilson says, "not as congeries of interests, but as a body of human souls, the least as significant as the greatest, not as you would calculate forces,

Figure 1.11   Woodrow Wilson
© Everett Historical/Shutterstock.com

but as you would comprehend life." Their imperfections, their obstacles, their rivalries, and their sympathies all factor in to our understanding and our work as students of politics. Their "errors of motive," "their confusions of purpose," "their habits as they live," each of these Wilson tells us are what we need to appreciate whenever we look at the human relationships that taken together form the politics in our lives.

"I do not like the term political science," a skeptical Wilson finished in his remarks delivered at the APSA's meeting in December 1910, just two years before his election as the twenty-eighth President of the United States. "I prefer the term Politics," Wilson says, the scientific mindset inadequate for the insight, sympathy, and close-up comprehension of politics' human relationships. "Follow the dusty roads," "observe the crowded homes," "heed the cry of the children as well as the silent play of the busy fingers that toil that they may be fed," Wilson recommends, sounding in his own way like the voices of those reporters and crusading investigative journalists of his day shining

---

[14] Ibid., 2.
[15] Ibid., 10.

light on the suffering of so many people in turn-of-the-century America. Shun "precise talk of phe-nomena" and instead "follow the lines of strain, of power, of suffering," Wilson encourages.

"We must look away from the piecemeal law books, the miscellaneous and disconnected statutes and legal maxims, the court decisions, to the life of men," Wilson insists.[16] To study politics, study people, and study the complexities and the realities of their lives, the "scattered and disparate elements." Study them "not as you would calculate forces, but as you would comprehend life," Wilson suggests.[17] Sympathy, Wilson says, is our keenest, sharpest tool in our toolbox as students of politics. "Sympathy is your real key to the riddle of life," Wilson tells us.[18] So too is casting as wide as a net as we can to understand politics as it relates to everything else in our lives. Art, history, literature, and poetry all are properly in the study of politics.[19] "Spread a drag-net for all the facts, and then look upon them steadily and look upon them whole" is our charge and our challenge as students of politics, Wilson tells us in his December 1910 speech, a flawed President in so many ways yet a scholar with a historian's instincts and temperament, and with a keen eye for the fullness and richness of the human experience as expressed in political life. His words here, less than his deeds less than two years later with his election as President, is part of what is to follow in the pages of this book.

---

[16] Ibid., 6.

[17] Ibid., 11.

[18] Ibid., 10.

[19] "I do not know how some students of politics get along without literature, as some of them make shift to do, without the interpretations of poetry or of any of the other imaginative illuminations of life, or without art, or any of the means by which men have sought to picture to themselves what their days mean or to represent to themselves the voices that are forever in their ears as they do their doubtful journey," he continues. Woodrow Wilson, "The Law and the Facts." *The American Political Science Review* 5, no. 1 (February 1911): 2.

Reading Is Essential

I read constantly, and I always have a book with me or something of some kind to read everywhere that I go. I pack books to read for even short trips, even though one of the first places I always like to visit when traveling are bookstores, especially used bookstores. I am happy to have built a small collection of books in both my campus office where I work and in my office at home, where I do most of my reading. I own the first editions of some of my favorite books, less with a collector's eye, and more as a reader and a writer who is always eager to better understand where some of my favorite authors' ideas began in their earlier works. I annotate and underline and highlight my books, sometimes in different colors of ink for each of the times I have reread them.

I also carry my phone with me everywhere I go. With it comes access to an e-mail account filled with articles and with links to these articles and stories that I have read over the years, as well as a constant stream of news updates, alerts, and all manner of items to read throughout my day. I read e-mail updates that I have taken the time to set up in Google Scholar about some of my favorite authors. Every time they discuss their work in the press or are quoted or cited in some of the online scholarly databases I work with, my e-mail pings and my phone buzzes with this latest mention or reference to them. When I visit bookstores and libraries, my phone gets more of a workout as I send myself e-mails with the titles of books that I come across, titles that I will put aside to come back to later if I am working on something else at the time.

I use my online calendar to keep track of many of the books and articles that I want to read later, moving the titles of those readings forward in my calendar when they appear if I am working on something else so that I can make sure to be reminded of them later. When I finally have the time, or can turn my attention to them, my online calendar reminds me of titles on my to-do list. I keep a bulletin board in my office that always has my latest to-do list of books, articles, and chapters tacked up in front of me, but my online calendar is what keeps me in the game, and I would recommend it to any reader or writer wanting to keep on track in their future reading.

I tend to read faster than I should, and I let my eye glance across a page looking for specific items or names or topics of interest. I am easily distracted by footnotes, and I am likely to stop, look up a reference in a footnote, find it, and read it before returning to the book or text at hand. I like to look up what other publications an author has written if it is the first time that I have ever read their work. I stop to talk with or share excerpts as I read with friends, colleagues, and students. I underline interesting passages with a pen or pencil and write annotations in the margins. I can easily spend hours even on the sunniest of days turning the pages in front of me, and I easily lose track of time when I am reading something especially relevant to the work and writing I am doing at any time.

I like to read when I am at home, and I like to read when I am out, especially coffee shops, libraries, and the like. I have always been able to read in places or settings that other people might find distracting. I like to find a comfortable table where I can have a cup of coffee and read while conversations and activity carry on around me. I write mostly in the mornings or late in the evenings on most days, but I can read almost anytime, anywhere. I especially love to read on airplane flights, where I can sometimes read through an entire book if the flight lasts long enough.

Figure 2.1

© kikovic/Shutterstock.com

I reread things all the time and I enjoy rereading every bit as much as reading something new for the first time. I reread to find items I skipped over previously or something missed in an earlier reading. I reread as a way of finding something that may not have been useful to me in my original reading but in reading another time, I can now connect with in a different way as I work on different projects. I am perfectly happy to sit down to read a book or an article, and then immediately read it again right there and then for a second time. I never read a book or article or chapter intending to reread it as soon as I am finished, but I am happy whenever it happens this way to read something right away again. I will sometimes reread a book immediately after finishing it, something I am apt to do especially when I read well-written works of biography or history where the descriptions and the details are so plentiful that I know I won't get as much as I can out of it unless I reread it again, right there and then, right after finishing it.

I never have time to read everything I want to read, and I regard it as part of my good fortune to enjoy the work I do so much that I never seem to have the time to read everything that I want to read. When I read, it rarely if ever feels like work. Time spent in the library pulling books from the shelves is time that I value above almost anything else I do in the work that I do. Tracking down articles and chapters is something I enjoy as much as anything I do in my work. I rely on my friends in interlibrary-loan services to track down some of the out-of-the-way works I come across, and I am always excited when an article or book the inter-library loan staff have located arrives either as an electronic scanned file or when a book arrives from another library.

Figure 2.2

© Don Pablo/Shutterstock.com

I read every day and I write every day, and I start Chapter 2 with my own experiences with reading because I hope that my readers will take to heart my sincere hope that this book can instill in some small way some of the things that I have learned as a reader and a teacher and a writer of almost thirty years in the field of political science. I start Chapter 2 with this discussion of my own reading, because I think one of the things faculty with their students and writers with their readers do too infrequently is talk about <u>how</u> they read. I know well from my own experience and from that of my colleagues that we are enthusiastic when it comes to sharing our experiences of research and of writing with our colleagues and with our students. When it comes to talking and teaching about reading, however, we tend to be far less explanatory of what it is that we do when we read.

Shelves of bookstores and libraries are filled with titles on how to write for just about every imaginable kind of profession and purpose. Novel writing. Mystery writing. Writing children's books. Theatrical and screen-script writing. Technical writing. Resume and letter writing. Even grant writing. Books of almost every kind can be found by the score on every aspect of writing. Bestselling books on grammar and punctuation popularize the genre. Books on writing are so popular that in most bookstores, it is a well-visited aisle with its own well-stocked shelves and even sometimes some of the tools-of-the-trade: blank journals for authors, writer's diaries, and such. I have my own shelf in my office of these kinds books that I have read over the years, and I turn to these from time to time when I am working with students on their writing or when I am myself thinking of different ways to approach the writing that I do. Very little, it would seem, is not written down somewhere when it comes to writing.

How we think about and understand the place of reading in the work that we do is something far less frequently the subject of books, or courses and curriculum. Few campuses are without well-staffed writing centers, but almost none boast or host centers for reading, where students in a similar way might find assistance from peers and from professionals with a passion for reading. Librarian colleagues will insist that this is the task of reference librarians, and that an information desk and library faculty offer this assistance and answer these kinds of questions. Well-skilled as these library faculty and resource specialists are to assist with the location of readings for specific assignments, the commitment, and the passion for reading, I believe, is the responsibility of faculty within our respective disciplines and within our respective fields. It is in our classrooms, in our discussions with students, in our work with our students, where the commitment and the drive of reading needs to flourish, not just in end-of-the-semester, beginning-of-the-paper literature reviews, but in the constant encouragement and attention to reading in everything that we do.

Writing, as I will discuss in Chapter 3, is a discipline-demanding and time-demanding work for which there is no shortcut. It is all about the time that we commit to it. It is the hours and days and nights and weekends that we hone our skill as writers. We learn the craft and we find our voice in writing over time, especially the more time we put into it. It is the same with reading. The more hours spent in our reading, the more mindful and practiced we are at it. It takes time. It is something we can all do better. It is something we get better at the longer we do it.

Figure 2.3

© Wutthichai Phosri/Shutterstock.com

Like writing, reading is something I feel is best when it is a part of the work that we share with the people around us. When I write, I talk about what I am writing. When I read, I also talk about it with the people who know me best, people whose questions help to shape and steer some of the same questions I ask and things that I work on. I often find myself picking up and reading (or rereading) a book chapter or article in response to conversations I have with friends, with students, or with colleagues. Their questions and the conversations we share together can pique my curiosity and prompt my reading in sometimes unexpected ways. I feel that when we talk about what we are reading with the people we know, it prompts us to put it into our own words, to give thought to our impressions and our learning in what we read. When we talk about what we are reading, it is an important part of being able to turn what we read on the pages in front of us into our own words and our own writing later.

Figure 2.4

© Kira Garmashova/Shutterstock.com

The sociologist C. Wright Mills tells us that writing is something best done when we have people around us who we can talk with about our work, and I would add that the same thing he says about writing is also something that can be said about reading. "I do not know the full social conditions of the best intellectual workmanship, but certainly surrounding oneself by a circle of people who will listen and talk . . . is one of them," Mills says in the closing pages of 1959s *The Sociological Imagination*.[1] Mills rightly tells us that any and all "discussion with friends," as he puts it, is fruitful as we think through and work through our writing and our research. Talking with others about our work while we are still completing it, these "informal interchanges" and "interludes of discussion among individuals," as Mills puts it, shape and to some extent help to guide our work.[2] I agree completely with Mills, and I think we need to do this whenever we can with our reading as well.

When we read, we need to talk with others about what we are reading just as much as we need to take our notes, and to annotate in the margins and underline in paragraphs of interest. Mills feels that taking clear, detailed notes whenever we read is crucial to the work and writing we do. "You will

---

[1] C. Wright Mills, *The Sociological Imagination* (New York: Oxford University Press, 1959), 201.
[2] Ibid., 198.

have to acquire the habit of taking a large volume of notes from any worthwhile book you read," Mills says. I agree with Mills, and I'd add that I prefer typing my own notes from a book or article when I am finished reading it into a Microsoft Office Word or Google Docs file that I can save on my computer and later search and use in whatever way I need.[3] Writing notes as we read is a "prod to reflection" and "a great aid in comprehending what you are reading," Mills says.[4] It allows us to get in the habit of writing and to experiment as a writer, as Mills puts it.[5] I agree completely, and I'd add that when we read something, it is just as important that whenever we can we <u>talk</u> about what we read.

When we talk about what we read with the people around us, I feel that we become more comfortable with working through what we read. When we read, it can be every bit as demanding as our writing, but by talking about it with the people we know best, we can put our thoughts out there to others, both to help us remember what it is we read as well as to try out almost a kind of rough-cut outline or first draft of sorts on what we read that can later make their way into the words we write. To the extent that you can explain what you are reading to someone else in a clear, easy-to-understand way, it makes it that much easier and likely that you can do the same in your writing. I feel that between taking notes as we read and talking about what we read with the people we know, we are better prepared to take what we read and make it work in our own writing.

I also feel that starting at the end with the bibliography and the works cited in endnotes, footnotes, and other references is something we need to become better for much of the reading we do in the study of political science. I sometimes liken this to a kind of reverse-engineering, this reading <u>backwards</u>, as it were, beginning with the bibliography and working through the references before reading the work itself. I think one of the most useful skills for readers in our field is to learn how to branch off and read the bibliography of an article or a book before we read the article or book at hand. I always encourage my students to start at

Figure 2.5

© Africa Studio/Shutterstock.com

the end of a book by thumbing through the bibliography. I find few students have ever been encouraged to do this. Even fewer have ever learned how to read footnotes and endnotes, much less how to write them in their own work. In the study of political science, students may very well not write footnotes or endnotes much themselves depending on either their preferences or the requirements of citation formatting, but if our students do not regularly get in the habit of

---

[3] I'd add that whenever I cite or write the references from my own typewritten notes saved as a Microsoft Office Word file, I still always will have a copy of the original text itself and have that page in front of me when I write, something easier to do if I own a copy of the book or if I have scanned and saved these page images for exactly this purpose.

[4] Wright Mills, *Sociological Imagination*, 199.

[5] Ibid., 197.

reading the endnotes and footnotes in those works they read, they may very well miss important material that can help them better understand the work at hand.

The footnote is the first thing that I look at on a page, and it is the first thing that I see when I open a book or begin reading an article or chapter. I am distracted easily by the footnotes, and I am eager to get a sense before I begin reading what the material and sources the author is drawing from to make their own argument. I talk with my students of looking first at the footnotes when we start our reading, letting us get a sense of the extent of the author's documentation and sources they are working with. I believe that learning how to begin with at least a short skimming of the endnotes or footnotes is something that opens us up as readers to sometimes look up other works or writings cited by the author even before we read the work at hand. It's there that sometimes we'll find the article by an author we have never heard until now, or that we might come across an article or chapter or even a book we have never discovered before now by the author whose work we thought we knew well. When I start with a book or article or chapter that I know has a well-referenced bibliography, I read through it before I do anything else to see how many titles I am familiar with, and what works I have read myself or that I want to read. It's a habit I have used for many years in my reading, and one I recommend to anyone able to see reading as far more a process of moving back and forth across a book or article or chapter than simple start-to-finish linearity.

When reading, we always want to make it easy for us to go back to find those ideas and thoughts that left an impression on us as we read them. I think one of the ways that we do this is by keeping the books we own organized by topic on the bookshelves. I know it seems like a simple idea, but I think it's helpful to keep the books that I own together by topic, helping to spur connections between titles as I look at one book and then remember a related idea or item that I want to look at again in a different book that is near the book I am looking at. Pulling books off the shelves in my own office or in a library or a bookstore is how I sometimes make those connections between books I might not otherwise put together. For the notes from my reading that I take and type up in Microsoft Office Word, Google Docs, or other searchable documents, and for the various copied and scanned files that I accumulate as I read, I like to give these longer names with as much information as possible that makes it easier to search later and find them on the computer when I am reading and writing my own work.

Keeping track of the notes we take and the files we accumulate as we read is one of the skills in reading that we can do better, and it is something that we get better at the longer and the more that we read and take notes of what we read. Being able to remember where something is that we have read and keeping our notes and documents from our reading organized enough so that we can go back to them easily when needed is something that we get better at over time. I feel it gets easier for me to

Figure 2.6

© Charlie's/Shutterstock.com

do the more that I work at it. Online search engines like Google Books and scholarly databases like JSTOR make it easier than ever for us to locate specific passages in books or articles that we have already read, but I think despite the ease in locating these snippets of text in the works we have read, it still is invaluable for the reader to take the time whenever possible to still locate this material in its original form. I still want to look at whatever it is in its original format. Even if I have a full-page of a book in front of me on the computer screen from Google Book, I still will almost always get the book so I can page through it more carefully and get a chance to see the author's work in its entirety.

When I wrote my recent book on the history of political parties in America, I spent hours walking up to the fourth floor of our library to read some of the letters and writings of George Washington, Thomas Jefferson, Alexander Hamilton, John Adams, James Madison, and others, all volumes published by Columbia University Press, Princeton University Press, and the University of Virginia Press as a part of the National Archives and Records Administration (NARA) National Historical Publications and Records Commission (NHPRC). I easily might have quoted these letters and writings from any number of works written by other authors or by contemporary works of history, but I found it useful to read these writings in these beautifully-edited, multivolume editions and cite them as such for my readers. I did the same for some of the records of early sessions of the Congress, looking through the multivolume editions of early Congressional records published by the Johns Hopkins University Press' *Documentary History of the First Federal Congress, 1789–1791*. I feel it is always worth taking the time to read a book or article or chapter in its original format, and it is also worth taking the time to page through the entire book or article, not just a passage or part of it.

The more we become proficient in taking notes in what we read, the more we are practiced in underlining and in keeping track of the things we read, the more well-organized we are in keeping our books together on our shelves, the better organized and readily accessible the electronic files of scanned documents and written notes that we assemble as we read, the more that we do all of this, the better we are at using these materials later when it comes to our research and writing. In that regard, having paper, pens, and a computer nearby to type up and keep track of our notes is always helpful.[6] I also suggest using your cell phone camera to send images of book

Figure 2.7

© aPhoenixPhotographer/Shutterstock.com

---

[6] I once regularly underlined passages in pages of books and articles using a ruler and pen, a habit I began as an undergraduate and still did as a graduate student. For that reason, I used to always have a good supply of clear-plastic rulers to underline and use when reading books. I now typically do much more writing of my own notes and

pages to your e-mail. I spend a lot of time in libraries, and I never am without paper, pens, and my telephone with its camera and e-mail when I need to be able to send written notes or images while reading directly to my e-mail. I'd add that some of the most important work that I do in libraries is coming across the unexpected titles that I find, usually by taking the time to look at books adjacent to the titles on the shelves that I have come there to look up and to read. I always regard it as a successful visit to a library when I have found not only the books I intended to locate in my visit to the library, but when I also have had the chance to find an additional title or two that expands my work.[7] I also find in my work that looking at additional titles by an author, even if the title itself may not be directly related to the specific topic I am reading about and researching at the time, can sometimes be useful material for later work.

I mentioned earlier that I regularly use my online calendar as an effective way of keeping track of readings, especially those that I come across in visits to libraries or when I am in bookstores or elsewhere, but don't have the time at that time to be able read. With these titles, I will place them some weeks in the future on my online calendar, so that when the date finally comes around that I have placed that title, I can either take the time to go find the book, or otherwise I can easily simply move that title forward in my online calendar to be reminded again in the coming weeks or months of that title. I have so many of these set as a part of my online calendar that the title of a book or article or chapter comes up on my online calendar almost every day, so it's a continual reminder of other readings and works that might potentially be of interest in any work I am doing at that time. If not, a few clicks of the keyboard and those titles are easily forwarded in my online calendar to remind me again. It makes it almost impossible for me to lose track of titles that I hope to look at, and I can easily add new titles to my online calendar with my phone when I am in, say, a library or a bookstore. I can just as easily delete these items if my interests have changed such that I no longer feel I need to look at an item that once seemed important for me to read.

I also might suggest from my own success in reading in using the draft feature in e-mail to keep track of future readings, especially those items and stories that I come across on newspaper websites and other sources but that I don't have the time to look at, at the time. I keep these items in the draft feature of my e-mail account, so that it is both fully searchable as I look up items in my e-mail as a part of my research, and it is easily accessible so that when I find the time, I can finally read through and then send to my e-mail account these items to be archived and accessible for future rereading and reference. I usually have hundreds of stories in my e-mail's draft-mode, so

---

thoughts on the pages of the readings I do, and write or rewrite some of these annotations directly into my writing or into my typewritten notes in Microsoft Office Word or Google Docs.

[7] "Put yourself in the way of random choice," Aaron Wildavsky tells us in a magnificent chapter on reading in his 1989 book, *Craftways: On the Organization of Scholarly Work*. "Try book stacks in libraries," he urges, "dipping in here and there to catch sign of what one may have missed." He also urges us to visit periodicals rooms in libraries to, as Wildavsky puts it, "rummage through journals in many fields" to find something that might be of interest to us. "Being a reader, that is, a person who loves to read, helps to randomize reading," Wildavsky adds. "One is more likely to pick up almost anything almost anywhere, and it is precisely in these unexpected places that the valuable example or reference is likely to appear." Aaron Wildavsky, *Craftways: On the Organization of Scholarly Works* (New Brunswick, N J: Transaction Publishers, 1989), 26, 27.

there is always work to be done. I especially like to catch up on some of this reading of my e-mail's draft-mode articles when I travel and don't want to take a large amount of reading with me. Much like the use of the online calendar to serve as a digital to-do list and reminder of works, the draft feature of articles and items gathered from across the websites and digital sources that I regularly read makes it less likely that I will misplace or otherwise lose track of these items that I want to take the time to read when I find the time to catch up on my reading.

I've spoken in several different instances to this point on rereading, and would simply say on this point that it's certainly helpful to be able to easily locate something that has been read in the past, especially when you are writing and trying to recall an example or quote to cite from something you have read. There is always something you didn't see when you read it the first time. I have said here that some of my rereadings of articles or chapters or even books happen when I have conversations that prompt me to want to look again at something I have already read. Rereading is something I am so accustomed to doing that I look forward to rereading an article or chapter that I've read before on the chance that it might include an idea or an item that did not make an impression on my first reading but can in a subsequent rereading offer just the right insight or perspective now.

Not everything we read, to be sure, is something we need to read a second time or more. But the more readily we pick up a book or chapter or article for a second time or more to refamiliarize ourselves with it, the more readily we can make it a part of our own writings in new and sometimes unexpected ways. The more we take the time to reread an article, book, or chapter for insights missed before or for materials not directly related to the questions and subjects we were studying at the time of our initial reading, the more we can find new ways to make use of items we have already read. I search my computer regularly for documents and materials when I do my work, and when I do these searches, I sometimes pull up files not relevant to my work in that moment, but which might be useful for me to look at it again either for another project or just for the enjoyment of looking back at something I had read and that I felt important enough to archive and save at the time. I always find these articles and readings that pop up unexpectedly when I am searching for something else in my own digitalized files to be some of my favorite rereading, and I put it aside until I find a break in whatever else I am reading or writing to return to it. I usually end up printing out a copy of these files, and will put them aside until I have caught up with whatever I am working on to return to look at them. Sometimes, I might delete the file if I think I've gotten all I will need from it and will not need it for anything again, but more often, I will check the filename to make sure it includes any additional information from my rereading to make it easier to find should I need to locate it again. I routinely update the filename of these digitalized and scanned files whenever I reread them, or even when I briefly look at them in passing when they turn up in whatever searches I might be doing.

For political scientists, it is important for us to always be as attentive and selective in the sources that we read and where we regularly turn to read and to learn about the issues we study. In the study of political science, books for both more general audiences as well as more specialized academic and scholarly titles are an important part of what we read. As a field with a broad public interest, especially during the campaigns and elections that draw so much attention by so many people, books on politics that are intended for more general audiences can be especially helpful and important for students of political science. I come across many of these titles in my visits to bookstores, in watching television news program featuring guest interviews with the authors of these books, and keeping an eye on the titles reviewed by the newspapers I read on a regular basis. Scholarly journals are certainly important for students of political science, and it is useful for us to regularly turn our attention to them. Like many things today, e-mail updates and alerts from these journals can be one of the most useful ways to keep up with the work being published in these journals. I have had success using such e-mail alerts and updates from some of the larger scholarly databases made available through my university's library. These table-of-contents alerts and e-mail updates of their latest issues from the publishers and websites of the academic journals themselves bring some of the latest scholarship and work our way.

I have had considerable experience with Google Scholar as both a search engine when I am looking for scholarly writings, as well as using the Google Scholar e-mail alert for authors or topics that I want to keep track of in my work and writing. Google Scholar e-mail alerts are every bit as user-friendly as Google News Alerts. As I read books, articles, or chapters, I will often set these Google Scholar alerts so that I can get reminders sent directly to my e-mail of any new work by these authors, or the references and citations to their work by other authors that, in turn, can take me to read those articles or at least save the references to return to read them later. Between the table-of-contents of new issues e-mailed from the websites of many academic journals, and the e-mail alerts from services like Google Scholar and others search engines, students of political science have some easy-to-use tools allowing them to cast a wide net across some of the most important and useful sources of scholarship in our field.

Figure 2.9

© tongcom photographer/Shutterstock.com

As a teacher and a writer of over thirty years in the field of political science, I am especially aided in the reading and the work that I do by some similar resources and tools that now allow me to be updated at almost every hour of the day by the news stories and analysis that I need as a part of my teaching and my writing. Thanks to the e-mail alert services from some of the newspapers and websites that I have set over the years as well as hundreds of e-mail alerts that I have set through Google News Alerts, *The New York Times'* My Alerts, and other services, I receive stories and news items within minutes of breaking events, some of which can be easily deleted, others archived for later searching or use in my e-mail, and those which I will then and there take the time to read and then to archive for future reference or to use later.

I begin my mornings almost every morning with the review of the overnight e-mail news alerts and search alerts that are a part of my e-mail in-box, especially the news alerts and daily summaries from several major newspapers that I have these alerts set up for as well as the hundreds of Google News Alerts that I have set up. I am constantly adding and deleting daily as new stories or items of interest to me arise, or as I decide that an alert set earlier on a topic is no longer useful to me. If I purchase a book in a bookstore or on Amazon or another Web retailer, I will use the trick of setting a Google News Alert on the book even <u>before</u> I have a chance to read it as it awaits atop one of my stacks of books in my office at home. It is a trick that I use to remind myself of the book once I purchase it, and if I receive enough alerts through my e-mail, it may motivate me to take it that much sooner from its spot atop one of my stacks of books waiting to be read. If it is a book with a larger national audience on the political debates and issues of the day, setting a Google News Alert before I read it lets me know as I make my way to finally reading book of the impact that it is having in the debates and discussions of the day.

Setting up a Google News Alert on a topic usually takes just seconds and these alerts, along with e-mailed alerts and early-morning daily summaries from several of the newspapers I read every day provide a first-look at the news stories and especially the long-form

Figure 2.10

© photobyphotoboy/Shutterstock.com

news analysis that I will often try to make the time to read later that day when I am at one of my computers to more carefully read the entire story. Through experience with these Google News Alerts over the years I have been using them, I have become accustomed to setting them up for individual reporters whose work I greatly respect. In a profession where these reporters can sometimes move from one news outlet to another, setting Google News Alerts to their name allows me to keep up with their work (and references to their work by other journalists) and never miss their latest stories and reporting on whatever topic or topics in the coverage and reporting of politics they are working on at any time. I long have encouraged my own students to find those journalists whose work and writing is so useful for their interests, and then make a point of following them either through e-mail alerts of whatever kind or by using sources like Twitter where most journalists today will helpfully post links to their latest stories and reporting.

With even just a few simple steps, political science students can easily tap in to some of the same news alert services and sources used by some of the most influential decision makers and officials in Washington, DC and throughout the country. Politico's Playbook is the most well-known of these early mornings, driving-the-day news sources, and Axios AM and others like it do an incredible job in summarizing stories from hundreds of sources to be read

Figure 2.11 The New York Times Building, Eighth Avenue, New York City

© Osugi/Shutterstock.com

on tablets and cell phones before the morning's first cup of coffee by thousands of readers. Twitter is every bit as useful for students of political science in customizing their news feed, and its continuous updating is for some readers of more use than sources like Playbook or Axios AM or even *The New York Times'* First Draft which arrives in my e-mail usually around 7:00 a.m. on weekdays and is my own personal favorite that blends both the outstanding long-form journalism and reporting of *The New York Times* with its up-to-the-minute reporting and summaries of that day's main stories.

In my early morning reading of these overnight e-mailed Google News Alerts and various daily-summary e-mails from a variety of sources, I have, as I have said, a favorite that stands apart from the others. *The New York Times'* First Draft that arrives around 7:00 a.m. weekdays is my favorite of these, and is one that I read in its entirety almost every morning. *The New York Times'* First Draft is the kind of journalism and reporting that I would urge to any of my students or readers of this book, especially in the age of digital-clutter and information-static. Over the years, I have also been partial to *The Los Angeles Times*, whose news updates and breaking-stories alerts provide for me a window into the political stories and breaking news in the nation's largest state. My own students over the years have heard me speak of *The Los Angeles Times* as a paper whose commitment

Figure 2.12 The Washington Post

© Nicole S Glass/Shutterstock.com

to award-winning, in-depth reporting helps to provide a useful perspective on the news to accompany the reporting of *The New York Times, The Wall Street Journal*, and *The Washington Post*.

Whatever your websites or news sources of preference, I would encourage every student of political science to regularly have e-mailed updates of at least one or more newspaper websites or services that features long-form journalism, the kind of in-depth analysis and reporting (often by multi-author teams for larger stories) that can cut through the static of the day's headlines to provide the insights and wide-angle lens perspective that only is possible with the expense and the investment of time, travel, and editorial guidance from newspapers like *The New York Times, The Wall Street Journal, The Washington Post*, and others. When I think of the reading we need to do in political science, I would advise students just beginning their studies to regularly read the works of long-form journalism in these or other nationally recognized newspapers still driving our national debate, even in an age where newspapers have faced all manner of advertiser and circulation challenges and competition.

I read all the time, almost anywhere and everywhere, and I read anything and everything that I think will provide for me the kinds of insight and attention-to-detail and in-depth information that I am seeking in my study of politics, whether I am trying to work through the history of the Whig Party, or I am trying to understand the latest budget negotiations and budget bills debated on Capitol Hill. I read widely, and I like to think that I also read wisely, that is, I take the time to get to know and become familiar with the authors whose work that I read. I take the time to look through their references and works that they cite and use, even before I read their work, and I take the time to talk about these works with people around me and to reread whatever I need to as I move from teaching to writing to simply watching the news or having a conversation with friends that prompts me to pull something out and read it again. I read wisely, too, in that I make every effort in a deliberate way to make sure that once I have come across a title that I want to read, it either goes into my online calendar where I can make sure I won't miss it, or I will secure a copy however I can to be able to read it then or in the future if I am working on something else at the time.

I keep careful track as best I can using e-mail archiving as well as various typewritten, searchable notes in Microsoft Office Word, Google Docs, or other scanned and digitalized documents of as much of what I read as I can, so that, in this day of digitalized document scanning, my campus office and the office in my home do not have filing cabinets that I sort back through in search of readings, but instead my files are electronically archived, mostly scanned into readily usable formats, accessible with a simple search, and available for easy reference or for the rereading that I value so much in the work that I do.[8] I have taken years to assemble a digitalized, searchable set of typewritten notes, scanned documents and files, and all manner of both online materials through my e-mail as well as files stored on my computers that I use for my research and my writing. If it is material that I use in my reading and research and writing on a regular basis, it is all but certain that it is in a digitalized document of some kind.

I don't have metal filing-cabinets in either of my offices, but what I do have are wooden bookshelves, shelves filled with the books that I have collected and culled and read and reread for years. I have my books in both of my offices arranged by topic on my shelves, as I have mentioned elsewhere in this chapter, so that if I am looking up a book for something that I am working on at that time, it's not uncommon for me to take a moment to also look at the titles on the same shelf and perhaps look at these other books as well. I appreciate

---

[8] Digitalizing or scanning of many of the documents and materials is a time-consuming part of the reading that I do, but I liken it to the time spent not too many years ago in photocopying materials into paper-copies. It is essentially the same process of scanning, only now instead of a paper hard copy that needs to be filed or stored away physically in filing cabinets or in storage of some kind, these digitalized files are easily stored and readily searchable on any of the computers that I use in the work that I do. It takes work in this digitalization and scanning but once completed, I have a copy that can be saved digitally and that saves an incredible amount of space. I also like to do one additional trick, that is, making .jpeg files from the digitalized, scanned materials of specific paragraphs or portions of pages, giving them titles when saved that allow for even more easy, effective searching when I am writing. Using the Microsoft Office Snipping Tool, I create smaller files with more specific content and with more specific titles. That way, I can search for files and find both the larger, longer files as well as the shorter, smaller .jpeg files with more specific sections. It makes it easier to track down readings and sometimes easier just to read a short item or passage rather than a longer article or chapter. I especially like to do this with full-pages of archived, digitalized historical newspaper images that lets me save just a specific story from a full-page newspaper that makes it easier to reread and to print out just that story on the page when I am rereading it or need it in my writing.

the feel of holding a book in my hand, of turning the pages and letting my eyes wander across the pages. Each book I own is a first rough draft of my writing (with my annotations in the margins of some books pointing me to new projects), and a kind of scholarly diary or journal of sorts (with a layering of underlining and highlighting for in my different readings), and each book is a conversation to be shared as well with the friends, colleagues, and students whose talks with me do so much to influence and shape both the books that I read (and reread) and the books that I have been fortunate enough to write myself.

Figure 2.13

© TTL media/Shutterstock.com

I close with a final word on a topic already discussed earlier: location. I think it matters where we read, even those of us like myself who can read almost anywhere. I have thought more about where I read today and where I have read in years past in writing this chapter than I have ever thought about it before. I think it matters that we think about where we read. I know that one of the few places that I can never read with the attentiveness I want to bring to what I read is near a television. Even when I am reading e-mails or other readings on a laptop or on my phone with a television on, the television will invariably trump whatever it is that I am reading.

I know some people do most of their reading on their Amazon Kindle or any of the popular e-readers and tablets on the market, and I myself have tried several times to adjust to life in the age of the e-reader. In the end, I think it is the physical feel and texture and weight of a book, the feel of the pages, the paragraphs and sentences in front of me, waiting to be underlined or marked up with my pen, the margins in a book with ample space to write notes and all manner of thoughts as I read, that even the best e-readers and tablets with all their note-taking and other features have yet to recreate for me as a reader.

When I think about the arc of my work as a student and now as a teacher and a writer, one of the most important things I have always been able to find are comfortable, well-lit places to do my reading. I can read almost anywhere, but I think being a mindful reader means being aware that reading sometimes requires us to form the habit of reading, and the place where we do that reading is important. Finding a place that is comfortable, well-lit, and making it the place where we do our reading is a part of our lives as readers and as writers. I spent four years as an undergraduate student at Illinois State University in Normal, Illinois, where I began to form some of my habits that I still follow as a reader to this day. I read almost every evening in those four years in the same area in the university's library, almost the same time of day, on an upstairs floor near some large windows looking out on the campus. I studied on a quiet floor upstairs in the library in an area whose shelves had many of the books that I needed for my major, and I eagerly read everything assigned by my professors.

Figure 2.14 Madison, Wisconsin

© EQRoy/Shutterstock.com

I studied political science as an undergraduate at Illinois State University, but what I learned more than anything were the possibilities that reading would create for me if I stuck with it and took the time to learn how to do it.

In graduate school, I did much the same thing. I usually did most of my reading in the Current Periodicals Room on the second floor of the University of Wisconsin-Madison's Memorial Library, a room where I spent years in graduate school reading the assigned readings for book-heavy graduate seminars, and then scoured the wooden shelves for the latest peer-reviewed journals and periodicals, many of which I regularly paged through that were outside of my field of political science. With its large tables and the high windows that let in the light of the changing Wisconsin seasons, I spent many an afternoon and evening at those tables in the Current Periodicals Room. I also regularly read in the high-ceilinged main reading room of the Wisconsin Historical Society, just across from Memorial Library, and I had an office in North Hall where I often read in the evenings as my doctoral dissertation neared completion. I especially liked Madison's coffee shops in the downtown area along State Street as places to read, and I still find myself drawn to coffee shops as some of my favorite places to read today.

I read constantly, and I make sure that even when I am on the shortest of trips, I always have something to read along the way. I always have a book with me in my car, and always have plenty on my phone to read whenever I go anywhere. I read as much as ever, and rereading holds a place of importance for me as I have grown more to appreciate less how <u>much</u> I have read than how much I have gotten out of what I have read. I underline and annotate, and I always have my pen, phone, and Post-it notes at hand. I take time to read through footnotes and endnotes, I send e-mails of page numbers and references from my phone to my e-mail, and fill Post-it notes with thoughts as I read. I read more and I enjoy more than I ever have in my life, I <u>never</u> have the time to read everything that I want to read, and I have several piles of books stacked precariously atop my shelves in my office at home that remind me every day of just how much more reading I still have left. I read every day, I write every day, I never have as much time as I wish I had to do both, and I do so ever more mindfully of just how <u>much</u> I have yet to learn in my reading and my writing.

Writing Is Everything

I write every day, and I always have some writing of some kind I am working on all the time. I edit and revise every day, and I write and rewrite every sentence, paragraph, and page as many times as it takes for me to feel that I have gotten it right. I spend hours cutting words here, trying out different words there, forming paragraphs, scrolling through pages, and working to make whatever it is I am writing as clear as I can make it. I know my writing is flowing well when I find myself pausing momentarily to grab a pen and a stack of Post-it notes to write an additional thought that has come to mind but will work either somewhere else in what I am writing, or will work in a different project entirely. I can read almost anytime as I said in Chapter 2, and I can write almost anytime as well, but I know in my experience that it is in the quiet early-morning hours of a Saturday or a Sunday morning or in the later evening hours when distractions wane is when I do some of my best writing.

I know from experience that leaning-in, bearing-down, and staying at my desk is going to always be worth it in the end when it comes to the writing that I do. I take the time to work through sentences, sometimes word by word, until what I am writing reads the way that I want it to read. I know that whenever I can't make a sentence, a paragraph, a page, or even a chapter read the way that I want it to read, I need to face it head-on with a willingness, if all else fails, to delete some or even all of it and start over. I am a better writer when I take the time to delete and start over sentences or even whole paragraphs or pages if I can't get them right.

I am most productive in my writing when I am patient, when I take the <u>time</u> to work with my words. I know that rough drafts and multiple drafts are where I do my best work as a writer. I am a better writer and a more productive writer when I take the time to <u>slow down</u> in my writing, to work back over my words carefully, to type back over words and sentences I write and rewrite. I say in all honesty, there is almost never any time I know of in my writing recently that I haven't been able to work through these moments simply by working.

I get that many writers are talented enough to be able to write a mostly finished draft in their first draft, editing if only for any grammatical and spelling errors. I am not one of these writers. I prefer to do almost all my editing and revisions directly on the computer screen in front of me, instead of working through multiple printed copies of drafts that I once preferred. I like to start at the beginning of the text whether it is an article or a chapter or

37

Figure 3.1

© untitled/Shutterstock.com

whatever I am working on at the time, and scroll my way through paragraphs that I think are mostly finished, looking for those sentences here and there that might benefit from editing. I do most of my editing directly on the screen, only occasionally pausing to print out a paper copy of the latest draft and work through it, pen-in-hand, line-by-line, on paper.

I write every day, and so I start Chapter 3, as I did with Chapter 2, with this introduction of my own experience and habits of writing, in the hope that some of these experiences and the things that I have learned about writing in almost thirty years of teaching and writing in the field of political science can be of some small help to readers of this book. I have taught and thought about writing for the better part of almost thirty years, and I have published five books, a dozen or more articles for peer-reviewed journals, and written chapters in edited volumes as well as all manner of annotations, correspondence, lectures, letters, and such that I hope gives me some experience to share in this chapter.

I am aware as I begin Chapter 3 of this book, that if there is any subject where almost everything has already been written about a topic, it is writing. With a seemingly inexhaustible popular interest in books on writing, titles covering every conceivable aspect of writing easily take up small aisles of shelves in even the smallest bookstores. I own a shelf's worth of these books myself, and I reread favorites like Stephen King's *On Writing: A Memoir of the Craft.*[1] I encourage my students to read King's *On Writing*, as well as another favorite of mine, Howard S. Becker's *Writing for Social Scientists: How to Start and Finish Your Thesis, Book, or Article.*[2] Roy Peter Clark's *Writing Tools: 50 Essential Strategies for Every Writer* is a special work in a crowded genre of hands-on, how-to-write books, and I turn to it from time to time whenever I want a refresher in writing in an effective and engaging style.[3] Kenneth Atchity's *A Writer's Time: A Guide to the Creative Process, from Vision through Revision* is one of the

Figure 3.2

© Peshkova/Shutterstock.com

first books of this kind that I picked up on my own back in my years as an undergraduate political science major at Illinois State University, and is a title I still keep on the shelf closest to my desk to this day whenever I need to glance through its pages.[4] I keep all of these books on the shelf closest to my desk in my office, and I can pick one up by just leaning across my desk whenever I am thinking about or am asked a question about the writing that I do.

I like to read about writing, and I am interested in the lives of writers. I enjoy visiting the historic homes of some of our more famous authors when I travel, and I feel it is always remarkable to visit the homes of authors to better appreciate the work they did in these places. Ernest Hemingway's home in Key West, Florida, or Rowan Oak, the Oxford, Mississippi home of William Faulkner, are popular tourist destinations in these towns, and tell us much about the public's fascination with the lives of writers and the writing that they did during their lifetimes in these places. I think of the day almost twenty years ago that I walked up the stairs at Hemingway's home (where he lived from 1931 until 1940) in Key West for the first time to the upstairs room in a converted pool house where he wrote in the mornings, his round table with a typewriter in the middle of the brightly-lit second story room set in the lush gardens of the home's backyard. I remind myself of the afternoon I spent sitting on the front porch of the New Hampshire home of poet Robert Frost and walking in the woods behind Frost's home. I think of her father's law offices on the second floor of a building in downtown Monroeville, Alabama, where Harper Lee wrote her masterpiece, *To Kill a Mockingbird.*[5] Every time I visit New Orleans, I walk to the French Quarter sidewalk in front

---

[1] Stephen King, *On Writing: A Memoir of the Craft* (New York: Simon and Schuster, 2000).

[2] Howard S. Becker, *Writing for Social Scientists: How to Start and Finish Your Thesis, Book, or Article* (Chicago: The University of Chicago Press, 1986).

[3] Roy Peter Clark, *Writing Tools: 50 Essential Strategies for Every Writer* (New York: Little, Brown and Company, 2006).

[4] Kenneth Atchity, *A Writer's Time: A Guide to the Creative Process, from Vision through Revision* (New York: W.W. Norton and Company, 1986).

[5] "Literary Laurels for a Novice," *Life Magazine* 50, no. 21 (Friday, May 26, 1961): 78.

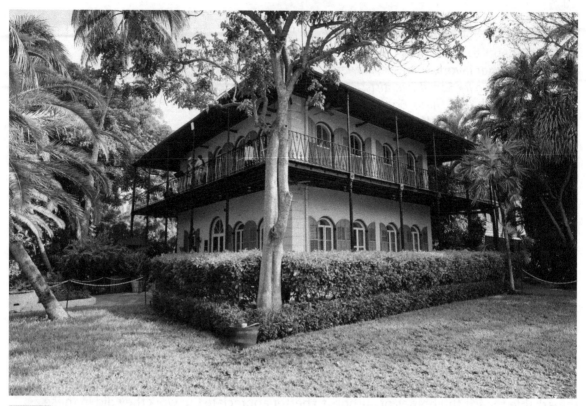

Figure 3.3   Ernest Hemingway's Home, Key West, Florida

© Robert Hoetink/Shutterstock.com

of the apartment where Tennessee Williams wrote *A Streetcar Named Desire*, and the building just around the corner (now one of my favorite bookstores in the entire country) where Faulkner lived during his years as a young writer in the Crescent City.

I write every day, and I talk about writing almost every day with the people who know me best, the friends, colleagues, and students who together help to keep me on my toes and motivate my writing. I think the <u>social</u> aspect of our writing is something that is not talked about enough when we think about writing. Every writer I know has their own stories of the friends whose words of encouragement and support push them through the difficult times in writing.[6] I quoted C. Wright Mills in Chapter 2, and I am quoting his same words here in Chapter 3 because I feel Mills offers what I know to be some of the best advice I can think of

---

[6] Tool #47 ("Recruit your own support group") of Roy Peter Clark's *Writing Tools* is one that I take to heart, and that I urge all writers to appreciate. Clark urges writers to "dismantle the disabling myth" of writing as isolated, solitary work. Someone must do the dishes. Someone must shop for groceries. Someone must cut the grass, and take out the trash. Writing means we almost always have an understanding family or friends willing to take on some of these tasks when we write, or at least to let us have the time to do what we do until we can get to these chores ourselves. Having family and friends to assist at every step of the process is something I take to heart, and something that I

in just a few words. "I do not know the full social conditions of the best intellectual workman-ship," Mills says in his must-read, closing chapter in 1959s *The Sociological Imagination*, "but certainly surrounding oneself by a circle of people who will listen and talk . . . is one of them."[7] I feel that Mills' words are as purposeful for us in writing as for any of the work we do, and I know that I experience almost every day in some way the meaningful and motivating influence of the friends, family, colleagues, and students I talk with.

I know that readers are accustomed to seeing the dedication pages of books, and seeing introductions of books filled with words of appreciation to family, friends, colleagues, coworkers, and others, and I know from experience that each one of these names is a sort of lifeline for the writer, someone with an ear to bend in those moments when we were working with our ideas on the page or someone who gave us help just when we needed it. I take the dedications and introductions of my books seriously, and I like to keep the introduction in mind throughout the project, to keep the people in mind without whom I would not be writing the words that I write.

I think that one of the constants that most books on writing talk about with their readers is encouragement to be mindful of the location where we write. I discussed the importance of place and of location in reading in Chapter 2, and I want to underscore the importance of <u>where</u> we write, something that is important to so many of those who teach and who write about writing. There is certainly a sentiment among these writers of the importance of finding creative solitude, as Carl Sandberg said.[8] I think of those writers who tell stories of writing in attics or window-less rooms, and I appreciate and respect this solitude some writers need. Some writers are happiest when they do their work in public, surrounded by the bustle of crowds and others writing or working on their own work. Some write with music. Others need a con-templative, meditative silence. Some write in rooms with spacious views, others are best when they are facing away from the window. Whatever the setting is, I think it is obvious to anyone who writes that it is always the preference of when, where, and how to write of the writer herself or himself that is more important than anything.

Figure 3.4

© Oleg Krugliak/Shutterstock.com

I think that writers make choices in everything that they do, and I spend a great deal of time especially in the consideration of the topic <u>long</u> before I put the first words on paper. I enjoy writing as much as I do, I think, because I have almost always written about topics only

appreciate Clark for pointing out. "In the real world," Clark says, "writing is more like line dancing, a social function with many partners." Clark, *Writing Tools*, 228.

[7] C. Wright Mills, *The Sociological Imagination* (New York: Oxford University Press, 1959), 201.

[8] Gladys Zehnpfennig, *Carl Sandburg: Poet and Patriot* (New York: T.S. Denison and Company, 1963), 233.

after considerable consideration of these topics and whether I am able to commit to it. I spend months, even years thinking about topics before I write on them, and I look at the topics from every possible angle that I can to consider what is different or unique that I can bring to the topic. I want to take as broad a perspective on whatever topic I settle on, and I know that this means that I will regularly write large sections of my projects that will invariably not make it past the final stages of my own editorial pruning.

Once I begin writing on a topic, I often will take such a wide perspective in writing that I am accustomed to writing entire sections or even chapters that end up not being published. In my doctoral dissertation, published as *Where We Live, Work and Play: The Environmental Justice Movement and the Struggle for a New Environmentalism*, I wrote an entire chapter on the history of environmental activism in the early 1970s that I ended up not including in my dissertation, in part, because I was eager to move from my opening theoretical chapters directly into the case studies I had traveled to research and write about in my dissertation research.[9] I unfortunately lost my only copy of that chapter as I completed my dissertation work and packed up my papers to leave the University of Wisconsin-Madison, but I know that I benefited from writing that chapter at the beginning of my doctoral work. I know that it gave me better perspective when I spent the time I did in the communities that I studied in Louisiana, New Mexico, and elsewhere.

In writing my 2014 book, *The Press in American Politics, 1787–2012*, I wrote a chapter on the history of the press in pre-Revolutionary America and a second completed chapter on the press in the War of Independence, but after putting the chapters together in preparing it for publication, I realized that these two chapters would not work as well as I had thought initially when taking the months writing both of them.[10] I left these two chapters out of *The Press in American Politics, 1787–2012* when published in 2014, but I still consider the work I did in writing them as invaluable preparation

Figure 3.5

© hareluya/Shutterstock.com

in my work in writing that book. I still have these completed chapters, and I may someday come back to these as projects to perhaps publish in a different venue.

"People are always saying to me in awed tones, 'think of all the *research* you must have done,' as if this were the hard part," Barbara W. Tuchman tells us. "It is not," she says. Tuchman laments those over-impressed by the research part of writing, and I agree with her that it is

---

[9] Patrick Novotny, *Where We Live, Work and Play: The Environmental Justice Movement and the Struggle for a New Environmentalism* (London: Praeger, 2000).

[10] Patrick Novotny, *The Press in American Politics, 1787–2012* (London: Praeger, 2014).

writing that is almost always underappreciated. "Writing, being a creative process, is much harder and takes twice as long," Tuchman says.[11] Research is seductive, Tuckman tells us. Writing is work.[12] It is sitting in our chair, at our desk, with our thoughts on what we gathered from our research, and it is deciding what is significant enough from our research to write about and what is not going to make the cut. It is picturing the reader sitting directly across from us at our desk.[13] It is the profane ("rearrangement, revision, adding, cutting, rewriting"), and it is the sacred ("rapture," "a moment on Olympus," "an act of creation"), and it is always twice as hard as almost anything else we do.

I appreciate Tuchman's words, and I agree with her that that writing is the most difficult part of most of what we do in the research in political science. I teach writing to my students with Tuchman's words, and I often think, when I read her words and talk about them with my students, of my own experience in writing *This Georgia Rising: Education, Civil Rights, and the Politics of Change in Georgia in the 1940s*.[14] I remember well the many months I spent reading documents and materials for *This Georgia Rising*. I traveled across the state of Georgia from local libraries in Macon, Savannah, and elsewhere to the Richard B. Russell Library for Political Research and Studies at the University of Georgia in Athens. I worked with documents at the Georgia Historical Society across from Savannah's historic Forsyth Park. I looked at whatever correspondence and materials of every kind that I could find, and I sometimes handled documents badly damaged and sometimes nearly destroyed by heat, humidity, and poor storage over the years. I was writing throughout my research on this book, and I always was writing on one or more of the chapters of the book. I remember well this was one of the last projects I have done with the old-style, reel-by-reel microfilm of many of these papers in Georgia from the 1940s, a growing number of which are available now in more readily accessible, searchable, digitalized formats.

I enjoyed the months of research in *This Georgia Rising*, and I talked with people from across Georgia and saw parts of my state by traveling to archives and libraries to access materials. I felt fortunate to learn the stories of change and courage by so many Georgians in the decade of the World War II. I enjoyed the writing as it took on a larger part of the work on the book, and the chronological format of the chapters lent themselves to a sequence of writing in the many months that took my archival materials from their handwritten-notes and black-and-white microfilm photocopies into the chapters I wrote on Georgia's 1940s. I changed the book's title in the closing months of writing it, from *The Day We Started to Fight* to *This Georgia Rising*, and I know it helped focus my editing and my writing in the homestretch of my final revisions. I certainly see in every way Barbara Tuchman's words on research and writing in everything that I write, but *This Georgia Rising* felt even more than most as I

---

[11] Barbara W. Tuchman, *Practicing History: Selected Essays by Barbara W. Tuchman* (New York: Alfred A. Knopf, 1981), 69, Italics in Original.

[12] Ibid., 21.

[13] "No writing comes alive unless the writer sees across his desk a reader." Tuchman, *Practicing History*, 58. I think picturing the reader and anticipating their questions, what I like to call doing the reader's work for them, is good advice by Tuchman and is certainly well advised to writers at whatever level of experience and expertise.

[14] Patrick Novotny, *This Georgia Rising: Education, Civil Rights, and the Politics of Change in Georgia in the 1940s* (Macon, GA: Mercer University Press, 2007).

Figure 3.6 Atlanta, Georgia

© Kragt Bakker/Shutterstock.com

prepared the manuscript for publication with Mercer University Press. I remember moving back and forth between microfilmed materials and the book's Microsoft Office Word chapter files, taking my writing down-to-the-wire in the final weeks of work. Finally, editing footnotes and deleting pages of the manuscript of *This Georgia Rising* to meet Mercer University Press' specifications felt every bit like Barbara Tuchman's thoughts on writing ("rearrangement, revision, adding, cutting, rewriting") in contrast to a research that I might have continued as long as I wanted with a seemingly inexhaustible amount of material and papers to read and research still further.

I think it is never too soon to start putting our ideas together on paper as soon as we start thinking through our subject, and I know it is sometimes the only way that we can discover what it is we are trying to look at in our research. Writing in this early, formative stage is some of the writing I enjoy the most in anything I work on, that first chance to put words on the paper and to see thoughts take form in the black-and-white of sentences and paragraphs. I want to let the words flow unimpeded as much as possible whenever I begin a project. I see it as a time to try out broad themes, to take chances and to take risks, knowing that most of what is written in this stage is going to be thoroughly edited if not entirely deleted as these thoughts and words take more shape on the page.[15] I like to try out lots of ideas whenever I begin my writing on something, and this relates to one of my favorite parts of one of my favorite books on the topic, Stephen King's *On Writing*. King tells us that writing is best when writers are willing to take chances. He tells his readers that to write, they need to do everything they can to let go of <u>fear</u>, whether it is fear of having not yet read enough, fear that there is more work that needs to be done before we start to write, fear of the sting of

criticism or rejection, fear of missing deadlines or of not having enough time to do everything a writer wants to do, or whatever that fear is for each of us. It is easy to put it off, to procrastinate, to come up with excuses, or to talk ourselves out of writing for whatever reason, yet putting all that aside and putting our first words on the page, however, much we may fear it, is what it is all about.

"Good writing," Stephen King says, "is often about letting go of fear."[16] It is only possible to start making sense of what we are thinking about when we get past that fear of putting those first words on the page. When we let go of fear, it lets us let the words flow from our thoughts on to the page. It is only then that we can see what our ideas look like not just in our own minds but as they will be read and seen by our readers. Letting go of fear lets us take chances, and it lets us begin to let the words take some form or shape in front of us, even if we have no clear idea what form or shape they will look like as we continue to write.

I think that once a writer gets a project started, the task at hand and the work at hand starts to get clearer. Paragraphs start to form, pages begin to pile atop one another, and soon enough it begins to look like something more than just a few scattered thoughts on the page. I believe in this early stage of the writing that it is helpful to keep the ideas all over the place and spilling out all over the page, getting ideas down as fast as they come to us. There's always time for editing and cleaning up the text later, but there's no time like the moment whenever I begin a project,

---

[15] I tend, too, to write many of these formative ideas on paper first, by hand. I like to write and to explore ideas on the computer screen, but sometimes, especially at the beginning of a project, I like the feel of a pen or pencil in hand as I try out new ideas on the pages of a legal pad or Post-it notes. Filling the yellow-pages of legal pads with these first thoughts and then typing them up can be a way of getting things started. Whatever it takes to get these ideas on paper early on is what you need as a writer, but I personally value the fluid and unstructured writing by pen or pencil on a legal pad, to try out a wide range of ideas and thoughts before typing them in to the computer.

[16] King, *On Writing*, 128.

especially in the beginning pages and stages of writing, to let the ideas flow from my fingertips. I think it is important that we allow the ideas to come to us as they come to us, and to be prepared only later, if need be, to delete whole sentences and sections.[17] I think at this early stage, it is important, too, for us to be prepared to see some of our earliest ideas take form and shape right away, sometimes much earlier than we might think possible. First thoughts are not always best thoughts, but I as a writer need to be prepared to see success right away in some of these early ideas, and not be too hasty in deleting or revising the writing that I do at the beginning in any project.

There is a time and a place for careful editing. I don't think the beginning is it. I want to get ideas down as quickly as possible on the page, while they are still fresh in my thinking. I want to take chances, and not be afraid to make mistakes. I can delete anything I write, and I can walk back ideas later. I want to push back against self-doubt, and to avoid too much self-criticism in early drafts.[18] In writing Chapter 1 of this book, I tried two very different ideas in writing the opening pages of that chapter, neither of which did want I wanted to do in setting the opening theme and tone of the book. My initial thought was to open this book and Chapter 1 in Washington, DC, what I feel is as appropriate of a setting as one can think of for a book whose audience is political science students.

I started writing an opening to Chapter 1 that drew from some of my own visits to Capitol Hill over the years. I sought to lay out some of the challenges and the issues that face us when we think about research in political science, especially the importance of making our work in political science relatable and relevant to the day-to-day realities of politics in places like Capitol Hill and elsewhere in Washington, DC. I spent days writing and then-rewriting paragraph after paragraph and soon page after page of thoughts from my visits in Washington, DC, over the years. I wrote pages of impressions of my time watching firsthand the day-to-day work of governing on Capitol Hill, and I hoped to use these opening pages of Chapter 1 to illustrate the down-to-earth ideas of dealing with political realities that I certainly want to encourage in this book.

After trying my hand at beginning Chapter 1 on Capitol Hill in Washington, DC, and feeling unable to get that opening of the chapter to say what I wanted to say, I finally gave in and

---

[17] I am mindful, of course, of the difficulties in deleting. What I do is open one or more documents that I will use to cut-and-paste these paragraphs or pages into, saving it usually with a long filename that makes it possible for me to more easily find it again and return to it at some point, and that way, I can delete the section without having to see such work as a waste of time with nothing to show. On the contrary, I am surprised by how often that something that is deleted and saved into a notes file or document ends up sometimes becoming relevant or used later in a project, or becomes the basis for an entirely new and different project. A sentence or paragraph that you think does not work out might very well prove useful later. A Microsoft Office Word file or Google Docs to put these deleted sentences and sections is something that we should start right away when we start any project, large or small.

[18] Tool #48 ("Limit self-criticism in early drafts") of Roy Peter Clark's *Writing Tools* is one that I think has some real use here. Clark invokes the idea of "harnessing the unconscious" in the "early stages of creation," of not casting too critical of an eye upon one's own work in these early, formative stages. Clark, *Writing Tools*, 233. I think this is helpful advice from Clark, this self-awareness, as Clark puts it, "of those moments when the critical voice shouts or whispers in your ear." I think that it can have a tremendous benefit for us as we write in these early stages of our work.

admitted defeat. I made the decision to start over and deleted the entire description of Capitol Hill. I mulled it all over, and decided to begin Chapter 1 with, of all things, a discussion of the importance of newspapers in the research and the writing that I do, and that I think should be important to all students of political science.

I feel in no uncertain terms that in a moment in time like today when we need to be ever more discerning and vigilant readers of the news, that the reputable, reliable newspapers of our time are a focal point of what we as political scientists should read and work with regularly. I already had well-thought out in advance that I would make the case in Chapter 4 that newspapers, the first rough draft of history, in the words of the late Philip L. Graham, are one of the most important primary documents when we bring a historical perspective to bear in our work.[19] I knew I intended to talk in Chapter 5 about how important I feel it is to read local newspapers whenever I travel and visit someplace. But I decided that I also wanted to open the first chapter of the book, and the opening pages of the book, with an opening homage to newspapers.

In this, my second attempt to begin Chapter 1, I poured out my thoughts and expressed my belief, page after page, of the importance of newspapers in all their many ways as a foundation of our reading and our work in the field of political science. I wrote at length of how important it is for political scientists to become regular readers of newspapers. I read newspapers throughout the day, every day, and I use them as much as any documentation and material in everything from classroom lectures to footnotes and references in much of my work. For the second time, though, I found myself staring at the screen with a furrowed brow, unable to convince myself that this discussion of newspapers would be the best place to begin a discussion of the reading, writing, and research stills for students in political science. I hadn't convinced myself that newspapers told the story that I wanted to tell in the opening pages of Chapter 1, so again I found myself back to square one, having a clear and relatively well-formed idea of what I wanted to say in Chapter 1, but still no clear idea as to how I would open this chapter.

Finally, on the third try, I was at last able to get the opening that I wanted for Chapter 1. I chose to open Chapter 1 with a discussion of the description (or definition, depending on how you want to look at it) of politics by Harold D. Lasswell in his 1936 book, *Politics: Who Gets What, When, How*.[20] Lasswell's well-known description of politics is the opening I settled on for Chapter 1. I decided to use Chapter 1 to give readers a broad overview of the book itself and to some of my thoughts on the study of political science more generally, so beginning the book with a discussion of Lasswell, and then taking the reader directly into a discussion of the book to follow left me satisfied that I finally found the right opening. Having worked as I did for days through

---

[19] I came across some debate by several authors during the writing of Chapter 4 regarding the words "journalism is the first rough draft of history," as they appear on the fifth floor of the Newseum in Washington, DC or some variant, as they are attributed to the late Philip Graham, the President and Publisher of *The Washington Post* and husband to the legendary Katherine Graham. Whether these words were first spoken or written by Graham or by editors or staff writers with his paper in the 1940s or first written or said in some way earlier than this by another journalist, I think it is certain that Graham *popularized* it a way that makes it less a debate of authorship than acknowledgement of his part in making the larger point.

[20] Harold D. Lasswell, *Politics: Who Gets What, When, How* (New York: McGraw Hill Book Company, 1936).

the first and second drafts, I felt that I had the opening I wanted finally on the third draft and one that I could build on in Chapter 1 and return to in later chapters of this book.

When I teach writing to my students and when I talk about it with my colleagues, I tell students and faculty colleagues that it is our job as writers to do the reader's work for them. When we write, we need to remind ourselves in everything that it is what we owe to our readers to give them the clearest, most straightforward writing that we can, and I believe the only way to do this is putting ourselves in the place of a reader when we write, listening to and reading our own words as they will be read by others.[21] I want to always do the reader's work for them, and I reread my words with an eye to rewriting them to always make them as clear, descriptive, simple, and straightforward as I can. Anticipating and answering questions even before they are asked, making the complicated sound simple, building pages where the writing flows from paragraph to paragraph, and bringing a certain lightness to the flow of our sentences, our paragraphs, and our pages is what we do when we do the reader's work for them.

Figure 3.8

© VGstockstudio/Shutterstock.com

"The advice often given to writers—first get your thought clear, and only then try to state it clearly—is wrong," Becker writes in *Writing for Social Scientists: How to Start and Finish Your Thesis, Book, or Article*.[22] I appreciate so much Becker's idea that writing is thinking, and I urge any writer in the field of political science at whatever stage in their own writing to look at Becker's 1986 *Writing for Social Scientists*. I have used Becker's quote that I cite above for years in my teaching and my thinking about writing with my students. I know it is a bold statement, and I know it is one that will not work for every writer. I reference it here in Chapter 3, to reinforce the idea that writing doesn't mean waiting until every idea is fully formed, but that writing is a crucial part and path to discovery for some writers, including myself.

"Writing need not be a one-shot, all-or-nothing venture," Becker says, telling us that an insistence on publication-ready polish is, in Becker's words, "entirely inappropriate" to those parts of writing, especially early in the project, when the task at hand is getting ideas on to paper.[23] I can tell you that there are ample examples of advice and recommendations in Becker's work sure to assist

[21] Barbara W. Tuchman says that writers need to be better listeners, and I think her words are apt in this sense when it comes to putting ourselves in the place of the reader. "Too many writers do not listen to the sound of their own words," Tuchman tells us. An "essential element for good writing" is, in Tuchman's words, "a good ear," especially when it comes to listening to the words they themselves *write*. Writers need to listen to the "sound" of their own prose, Tuchman says, something that she says not enough of them do, calling it "one of the failings" of writing in general. Tuchman, *Practicing History*, 16.

[22] Howard S. Becker, *Writing for Social Scientists: How to Start and Finish Your Thesis, Book, or Article* (Chicago: The University of Chicago Press, 1986), ix.

[23] Ibid., 14.

even the most confident writer in making improvements to their work. I feel that some of my best work as a writer comes at the beginning of a project, when I am beginning to have a sense of what I want to look at in general, but no real specific idea of where I am going to end up or what I am going to find. I move sentences and sections around quite a bit at this stage in my writing, often cutting-and-pasting sentences from one place to another to try out different juxtapositions and combinations of ideas until I get the sequence and structure that starts to work on the page for me.

"I do not know what I think until I have tried to write it," Aaron Wildavsky says in his 1989 book, *Craftways: On the Organization of Scholarly Works*. "I write to find out what I know," Wildavsky tells us. "I always hope to learn more than was in me when I started," Wildavsky adds, in line with the idea that writing is a form of thinking. "Few feelings compare with the exhilaration of discovering a thought in the writing that was not in the thinking," Wildavsky says in *Craftways*.[24] I think a thought-in-the-writing-that-was-not-in-the-thinking is a beautiful, almost poetic idea, and I know it is one that speaks to the belief that I share with Wildavsky.

---

[24] Aaron Wildavsky, *Craftways: On the Organization of Scholarly Works* (New Brunswick, N J: Transaction Publishers, 1989), 9.

I believe, as Wildavsky does, that writing is discovery. It is thinking. It is surprising yourself by sometimes being able to put on to paper and to say in words on the page more than you thought you knew.[25] I agree with Wildavsky, and I accept fully his idea that writing doesn't always mean waiting until our ideas are fully formed to put them on to paper.[26] Writing our earliest drafts before we know even what data or documents we are going to draw from and dive into is sometimes the only way that most political scientists are ever able to see what they will end up doing in their writing. For some political scientists, the only way we know what we need to read and what else there is to write is to begin writing, right away.

I know that some writers will do a diagram-style outline of whatever it is they are writing, sometimes posting on dry-erase boards or bulletin boards outlines of their ideas in whatever they are writing. I <u>do</u> use a bulletin board to keep track of some of my readings, as I discussed in Chapter 2, but my digital, on-line calendar is where I keep track of most of these readings. I do far less outlining in my writing than some writers, but I do use Microsoft Office Word files or Google Docs to try out a host of different ideas, less an outline than a series of thoughts and topics I hope to cover in a project. I update these, especially the ones on Google Docs, with my phone whenever I am stuck somewhere and I am struck by an idea or thought I want to include.[27] I think of Robert Caro's office in New York City where he does his writing by typewriter, with one of its walls covered with notecards and diagrams, right next to the desk where Caro writes. I think, too, of Faulkner's home, Rowan Hill, in Oxford, Mississippi, where visitors can to this day still see the outlines of some of his storylines written in the novelist's own hand on his home's walls. I do not write with a bulleted-outline, but I do put many ideas into my various Microsoft Office Word files or Google Docs, including notes from readings and quotes, many of which I hope to be able to summarize and put into my own words when I do my writing.

When I work with my students, two items I spend some time talking about at some length are paragraphs and paraphrasing. When it comes to paragraph structure, I encourage my students to be mindful of the form and format of their paragraphs. With occasional exceptions, I hesitate to ever begin the paragraphs I write with a quotation, and if I do, I like to make that quote in the paragraph's beginning to be a <u>main</u> theme that I call-back to throughout the paragraph.

---

[25] Ibid., 4.

[26] "Only by writing down what one thinks one knows can one figure out whether one knows it and what one does not yet know," Wildavsky tells us elsewhere in *Craftways*. Aaron Wildavsky, *Craftways: On the Organization of Scholarly Works* (New Brunswick, NJ: Transaction Publishers, 1989), 30. Tool #41 ("Turn procrastination into rehearsal") of Roy Peter Clark's *Writing Tools* is useful to mention here. Clark urges writers to "draft sooner," and he cautions that *over-researching* a topic make only delay writing and make it sometimes tougher to start. "Write earlier in the process," Clark counsels, "so you discover what information you need." Clark, *Writing Tools*, 203. Writing earlier than you think you can, Clark advises, is important so that these early drafts can "drive you to additional research," something that Clark discusses later in Tool #44 ("For big projects, save scraps others would toss") in his *Writing Tools*.

[27] I wrote in Chapter 2 that I use Google Docs when I take and type up notes from my reading. I also use Google Docs to write whenever I find myself away from the computers where I do my writing. I find Google Docs to be easier than bringing a laptop computer to a coffee shop or even a library if I am going to do some reading in one of those settings, and I want a way to take notes and to write. With my phone and with Google Docs or any other digital on-line document, I can tap the screen once and immediately begin scrolling and writing thoughts and even full paragraphs to be edited into my writing.

I also almost <u>never</u> finish a paragraph with a quotation, or even with a reference or a footnote. I always make a paragraph's last sentence one that brings together the paragraph with my own analysis, and flows for the reader into the next paragraph.

When it comes to paraphrasing, this is something that I talk with my students about at some length. I spend time with my students encouraging them to look for ways of summarizing and putting into their own words some of the quotes they cite in their work, always mindful of <u>still referencing</u> these sources as if it were a quote directly sourced. I work with students to get them to <u>own</u> their ideas, as I like to say, to rely less on quoting, especially quoting in the first or the second sentence in a paragraph. I talk and teach them in every way I know how of how important I believe it is for them to put enough of themselves and their own words into each paragraph they write that the beginning sentences and the ending sentences allow the reader to clearly see their analysis and explanation of the topic at hand.

Figure 3.10

© Pressmaster/Shutterstock.com

"Talent is not a rare commodity," Atchity says in *A Writer's Time: A Guide to the Creative Process, from Vision through Revision*. "Discipline is."[28] I know of few words in my almost thirty years of writing as a political scientist that I use more often when I talk and teach my own students of the importance of writing in the work we do. I speak from the heart when I share these words from Atchity, because I remember exactly when and where I was when I first came across Atchity's words. I was studying as an undergraduate major in political science at Illinois State University in Normal, Illinois, and I knew that writing was something that I wanted to do more seriously. I knew I enjoyed writing as a political science major, and I was eager to learn more about writing, so I set out to our campus bookstore, and I spent some time looking through the shelves in their section with books on writing, until I found a somewhat nondescript title that for whatever reason caught my eye and held my interest.

I read, and reread, Atchity's *A Writer's Time* over the next year or so, as I worked to build my confidence and my skill as a writer. In only a few months' time or so from that purchase, I took advantage of the first of several Summers when I was in college to continue the writing I had done on papers that I had written for classes during the previous school year. In the Summer before I left the familiar comforts of Normal for the University of Wisconsin-Madison, I devoted one last Summer to hone my writing skills. I worked on editing and revising ½ dozen or so papers that I had written for my various classes, as well as working on several papers that I wrote more for the practice of my writing skills than anything else. Finally, at the end of that Summer,

---

[28] Atchity, *A Writer's Time*, xvii.

I remember taking those papers I had worked on that Summer to the Illinois State University printshop, where I had them bound with a cover that gave it the feel of a small book. I started in that moment on a path that had begun improbably, as so many such journeys do, with a small act, namely that purchase of *A Writer's Time*, a book that made a great impression on me at the time and gave me a lifetime's advice I still think upon to this day on the commitment and discipline I need to do the work I do.

Taking to heart Atchity's talent-is-not-a-rare-commodity-discipline-is, I tell my students that the writer is only as successful as their self-discipline, and their willingness to take the time and to commit the time it takes to succeed in their writing. I firmly believe in every way that writing is a creative act, and as such, it is impossible to <u>force</u> these moments. When we will be at our most creative and imaginative in our work, the <u>timing</u> of these moments, if you will, is out of our hands. I know from my experience, and I know that every writer with any success shares this same experience, that creativity is impossible to anticipate or predict. We may wake up early on the quiet of a Saturday morning or begin the week bright-and-early on a Monday morning with all the intentions of writing, but a cleared-off desk, a cup of coffee, and a cursor blinking on the screen of the computer in front of us is not going to conjure up the words if they are not there. We may instead end up our day in the afternoon feeling exhausted and worn down, only to turn to our writing and unexpectedly see that creative impulse appear when we least expect it, and watch the words flow easily with very little predictability or way to anticipate when these moments might arrive. I <u>know</u> from experience that I <u>never know</u> when I am going to have those moments when the words come clearly and creatively with seemingly little effort or energy needed.

I think that our writing is impossible to anticipate or to predict because it is a creative act. We cannot compel these moments or force creativity. It keeps to its own schedule, and it keeps its schedule to itself. Like artists or musicians who might be moved whenever the spirit stirs them to create or to compose in those unexpected moments when they least expect it, writers need to be always <u>ready</u> for those moments where ideas creatively appear on the scene. I feel our willingness to put the time in, puts us in the position of being more likely to take advantage of these moments of creativity. I like to share with my students the words of the French chemist and biologist Louis Pasteur, who told his audience in a December 1854 lecture delivered at the Universite Lille Nord de France, "*Dans les champs de l'observation, le hasard ne favorise que les esprits préparés*," or in a rough translation to the simple sentiment, "chance only favors the mind which is prepared."[29] I see this as related to so much of the work we do as teachers and researchers and writers in political science, but I think it is in the work we do as writers especially were this is especially apt.

I feel, too, that even though writing itself as a creative act that is impossible to force or predict, I, as a writer, know from my own experience that there is always something to be done. I tell myself that there is <u>always</u> some part of what I am writing that needs to be edited or proof-read, and I remind myself that there is always some portion of whatever I am writing where I want to review my sentences and paragraphs to incorporate a change of wording or additional sentence or two that I can use to make my point more clearly.

As writers, we need to be mindful that even when our creative juices are not flowing to us in our writing at a given time, that there is still something that we can do in our writing, some pages or paragraphs that need our attention while we hope that those creative moments burst out on the page. I feel that the more time we work on these in-between parts of our writing, the more we will be prepared ("chance only favors the mind which is prepared") for those moments when creativity arrives. I believe that the more time we take to work on these somewhat more mundane details in our writing, the greater the likelihood we will be struck by the creative impulse and find ourselves unexpectedly pouring out the words onto the page.

Tending to the words we have already written with our editing, our rereading, our review of what we have written, I believe, is a very useful way of creating the right circumstances and the right conditions for those bursts of creativity to happen on the page. I know it is just as likely to happen when we are driving our car, dropping off mail at the Post Office, or standing in line at the grocery store, and I believe for that reason, that the writer needs to always be prepared

---

[29] Rene Vallery-Radot, *The Life of Pasteur*, trans. from the French by Mrs. R.L. Devonshire (New York: Doubleday, Page and Company, 1923), 76.

Figure 3.12

© Kitamin/Shutterstock.com

either with their phone to send themselves these thoughts, or with other materials to capture these thoughts as they come to us.[30] I always have a legal pad in my car for just such purposes, and I keep them handy anywhere else where I might have these thoughts come to mind when I am not anticipating or expecting them.

---

[30] Good ideas in writing "seem to come quite literally from nowhere," Stephen King tells us in *On Writing*, "sailing at you right out of the empty sky." "Your job isn't to find these ideas but to recognize them when they show up," King says. King, *On Writing*, 37. I cannot tell you how many times I experienced these epiphany-like moments myself, in some instances in rather extraordinary ways. I recall one particularly memorable experience, one that I share with my students, of driving my car just outside of Santa Cruz, California, at the end of several months on the road completing fieldwork for my doctoral dissertation. I was driving along a crowded road with a large tractor-trailer in front of me on the road, when several ideas came to me that I had been struggling with as I finished up my fieldwork. I reached for a legal pad and pen on the passenger seat, and hastily scribbled some of these thoughts as I drove, keeping a careful eye on the truck directly in front of me. My intent in visiting Santa Cruz had been to spend several days there to relax after finishing up my fieldwork, and instead here I found myself on an unfamiliar road, several thousand miles from home, doing my best to write down thoughts on a legal pad that might help bring together much of what I had been working on in my doctoral research for months. Today, if I find myself driving, I am more apt to pull off the road into a parking lot, tap the ideas out on my phone, and then return to my drive.

I tell my students that good writing <u>challenges</u> the way you think, and I tell them that great writing <u>changes</u> the way you think. I tell them that great writing is writing that <u>changes</u> us. It changes the reader. It changes the writer. It makes a difference. I tell them that their job as writers is to do their readers' work for them. I tell them that I agree with Stephen King when he says that reading is the creative center of the life of a writer.[31] I tell them that their choices as writers are to either make the complicated sound simple in their writing, or to make the simple sound complicated. I urge them to read one of my favorite short articles on writing, written specifically for political scientists, published by Thomas E. Cronin in a 1986 issue of *News for Teachers of Political Science*, a publication of the American Political Science Association (APSA).[32] I share Cronin's article with them, and I urge them to take to heart his advice for political science students hoping to take the writing component of their studies more seriously.

In a six-month time between October 1917 and April 1918, a young Hemingway spent his days and nights as a reporter for *The Kansas City Star*, traipsing through the city's police precincts, the Kansas City General Hospital, and anywhere else he could find the latest story for his paper. It's a time when Hemingway honed some of the skills of writing that lasted a lifetime for the novelist, with at least four or five of his novels as well as a dozen or more short stories all including some references to the reporting and stories he covered in his six-month stint for *The Kansas City Star*. Hemingway's largest collection of his personal papers, preserved for posterity today in the John F. Kennedy Presidential Library's Hemingway Collection, includes a copy of *The Kansas City Star* style guide used by Hemingway during his time in Kansas City.

The Kansas City Star's style guide, the novelist later said in an interview published in that paper in November 1940, were "the best rules I ever learned in the business of writing." "I've never forgotten them," Hemingway said in his interview published in *The Kansas City Star* in November 1940 of that paper's style guide and its strictures for accuracy, brevity, and clarity for its reporters.[33] Its prose, punctuation, and style guidelines for reporters— "use short sentences," "use vigorous English," "use short first paragraphs," "be positive, not

---

[31] King, *On Writing*, 147.

[32] "Outline, outline, outline," "Write with voice and power," "Write, write, then revise, revise, revise," "Omit unnecessary words," and "Vary the length of sentences and paragraphs, and vary how you begin sentences" are some of the subheadings for topics addressed in this essay, one I am happy to cite here from its original published by Cronin in *News for Teachers of Political Science*. Of the many topics covered by Cronin, 2 are of relevance to topics covered in my own Chapters 2 and 3. First, the discipline that is at the heart of the writer's work is discussed by Cronin. "As in the mastery of any ability, writing . . . requires self-discipline," Cronin says. No shortage of references to the discipline ("use time effectively . . . and ruthlessly stick to a schedule") and to the demands ("this is often like being sentenced to solitary confinement") and to the difficulties ("demanding, exacting, lonely, and often painful") it takes to write abound in Cronin's essay. Second, Cronin's closing thoughts in his essay are on the importance of *reading*. "If you want to become an effective writer, seek out the best," Cronin says. He encourages his readers to "adopt some of the best writers as remote mentors" and to "read their earlier works." "Able writers," Cronin tells us, "not surprisingly are constantly reading and learning from able writers." Thomas E. Cronin, "The Write Stuff," *News for Teachers of Political Science: A Publication of the American Political Science Association* 49 (Spring 1986): 1–4.

[33] Charles A. Fenton, *The Apprenticeship of Ernest Hemingway: The Early Years* (New York: The Viking Press, 1954), 34, 269.

negative," "eliminate every superfluous word," "avoid the use of adjectives," "try to preserve the atmosphere of the speech in your quotation"—impressed themselves on a young Hemingway and most certainly remained a touchstone for his lean, spare writing style for years to follow.

Of all the lessons shared throughout his life in interviews and in his letters and correspondence with other authors asking for his advice, Hemingway's most enduring idea from his days as a young reporter for *The Kansas City Star* through his years as a Nobel Prize–winning novelist is rewriting. "I always rewrite each day," Hemingway told George Plimpton in an interview for *The Paris Review* in the Spring of 1958, words that echoed his many conversations and correspondence and talks about his writing over many years. "When it is all finished, naturally you go over it," Hemingway told Plimpton in an interview in the Havana suburb of San Francisco de Paula.[34] "Getting the words right," Hemingway said.[35] It is the great pains that he took in laboring carefully over every sentence and every page that is as remembered to this day as much as any part of Hemingway's legacy as a writer.

"I write every morning as soon after first light as possible," Hemingway told Plimpton in 1958s *The Paris Review* interview in San Francisco de Paula. "There is no one to disturb you and it is cool or cold and you come to your work and warm as you write."[36] I think of an eighteen-year-old Hemingway writing and rewriting his copy at all-hours in the newsroom of *The Kansas City Star*, or the writer fifty years later speaking with Plimpton in his home near Havana, standing at his desk in the mornings, pencil in hand, pages of handwritten text carefully stacked under a paperweight on Hemingway's desk to keep them from fluttering in the breeze from the window in front of him, standing and struggling with each sentence and each page, as Hemingway himself put it, "getting the words right." Hemingway's early willingness to carefully craft everything he wrote, "even the one-paragraph news story," in the words of *The Kansas City Star*'s Assistant City Editor C. G. "Pete" Wellington, continued through the final years of his writing as Hemingway worked every day with his words on the page in front of him.

I think there is something to learn in the life and in the writing of Hemingway for every political scientist, and I think that we as political scientists can learn something from the novelists like Hemingway and others who dedicate their lives to writing the simple, sparing sentences that I think we ourselves very much want to write in political science's prose. The discipline of writing every day, the discipline of rewriting everything we write and of doing so every day, the discipline of deleting and starting over and sticking with it until we get the words right, and, perhaps most of all, the living of a life outward, filled with experiences and friendships that the writer can bring back to their work, I think all of this is something can inspire political scientists whose work it is to take the mostly mundane affairs of government and enliven them in the words we write.

---

[34] Ernest Hemingway, "The Art of Fiction," *The Paris Review* 18, (Spring 1958): 66.
[35] Ibid., 67.
[36] Ibid., 66.

Figure 3.13 Ernest Hemingway's Home, Key West, Florida

© travelview/Shutterstock.com

Tempting as it may be to allow Hemingway to have the last word in Chapter 3, I instead take these last few paragraphs and pages to connect with the words of William Strunk, Jr. and E. B. White. When a yellow-color dust-jacked title appeared in bookstore windows and on store shelves in April 1959, few if any would have ever imagined it would become one of the most admired and celebrated books on writing of its time. E. B. White's stature as editor of *The New Yorker*—as well as the author of children's classics *Stuart Little* and *Charlotte's Web*—lent immediate interest to the Macmillan Company's first printing of *The Elements of Style* in April 1959. The essence of Strunk and White's *The Elements of Style* is simple enough, and that is simple, specific, straightforward writing.

Seventy-one pages in that first printing of the first edition in April 1959 of *The Elements of Style* underscored eleven principles of simplicity in composition, including: "Make the paragraph the unit of composition," "Use the active voice," "Use definite, specific, concrete language," and "Omit needless words." *The Elements of Style* underscored an additional twenty-one principles of simplicity in style, among them: "Write in a way that comes naturally," "Revise and rewrite," "Do not overwrite," "Do not overstate," "Avoid the use of qualifiers," "Be clear," and "Do not take short-cuts at the cost of clarity."

"If those who have studied the art of writing are in accord on any one point, it is on this: the surest way to arouse and hold the attention of the reader is by being specific, definite, and concrete," Strunk, Jr. and E. B. White say in 1959s *The Elements of Style*, in a passage from their Elementary Principle 12 of composition ("Use definite, specific, concrete language") that is as relevant as ever. "The greatest writers. . . . are effective largely because they deal in particulars and report the details that matter. Their words call up pictures."[37] Even more to-the-point is their Elementary Principle 13 of composition ("Omit needless words") where their plea for brevity, boldness and clarity holds: "Vigorous writing is concise. A sentence should contain no unnecessary words, a paragraph no unnecessary sentences, for the same reason that a drawing should have no unnecessary lines and a machine no unnecessary parts. This requires not that the writer make all his sentences short, or that he avoid all detail and treat his subjects only in outline, but that every word tell."[38] "63 words that could change the world," as E. B. White said in his Saturday, July 27, 1957 article in *The New Yorker*.[39] In those 63-words quoted in White's 1957 *The New Yorker* article that began it all and in Elementary Principle 13 in 1959s first printing of *The Elements of Style* and in all of its subsequent printings and editions to this day, it is a book well-worth our time in reading and rereading in its short, simple, useful plea for brevity and clarity in writing.

I read every day, I write every day, and I rewrite everything. I am always excited when authors whose work I admire and respect either discuss the writing they do in interviews, or when they take the time to write about the writing they do. I think talking about the writing I do is the most important part of the writing that I do, and I try not to talk about it too often or for too long or too much with family and friends, but I find even those snatches of conversation here and there about the writing I am working on with the people in my life that matter the most to me motivates and moves me along in more ways than they might ever imagine when I am back at my desk, picking up where I left off. I have a lifetime's worth of lessons still left to learn in the time I have left in this life when it comes to the writing I do, even though I know there is no secret to it, there is no trick to it, there is nothing else to it except to keep at it every day.

---

[37] William Strunk, Jr., *The Elements of Style, with Revision, an Introduction, and a New Chapter on Writing by E. B. White* (New York: The Macmillan Company, 1959), 15–16.

[38] Ibid., 17.

[39] E. B. White, "Letter from the East," *The New Yorker* 33, no. 23 (July 27, 1957): 41.

There Is Nothing New In the World Except the History You Do Not Know

"The past is never dead. It's not even past," William Faulkner's character Gavin Stevens tells the audience in Act 1, Scene 3 of 1951s *Requiem for a Nun*.[1] "There is no present or future—only the past happening over and over again—now," Eugene O'Neill's James Tyrone, Jr. says in Act 3 of his *A Moon for the Misbegotten*.[2] The past is there and then, and it is here and now. It is a foreign country, but one that is never that far away. "Of all the bromides about the past," the late Clifford Geertz tells us, "that it is prologue, that it is a bucket of ashes, that it is another country, that it is not even past, that if you don't remember it you are condemned to repeat it, that it is the debris that piles up in front of us as we back into heaven, about the only one that comes to much as usable truth is Kierkegaard's, 'Life is lived forward but it is understood backward.'"[3] Faulkner. O'Neill. Geertz. Kierkegaard. I take this title's chapter from the words of a keen and avid reader of history, the thirty-third President of the United States, Harry Truman, but I know of no words more apt than those of Faulkner and O'Neill to open Chapter 4.

I bring a historical perspective to everything that I study and teach and write about as a political scientist. I think about almost everything that I study and teach and write about from the perspective of history, and I remember a childhood where history was a part and a presence in my life from an early age. Vacations with my family always included visits to national parks, historical sites, and museums everywhere we traveled, and I took an interest at a young age in archaeology, which almost became my major when I began my studies as an undergraduate at Illinois State University. I had done some summer archaeological digs in high school near where I grew up in Southern Illinois at the Cahokia Mounds State Historic

---

[1] William Faulkner, *Requiem for a Nun* (New York: Random House, 1951), 92. This same line—"The past is never dead. It's not even past"—is in Act 1, Scene 3 of *Requiem for a Nun's* 1959 adaptation of Faulkner's novel to the stage by Ruth Ford, *Requiem for a Nun: A Play from the Novel by William Faulkner, Adapted to the Stage by Ruth Ford* (New York: Random House, 1959), 33.

[2] Eugene O'Neill, *A Moon for the Misbegotten: A Play in Four Acts* (New York: Random House, 1952), 128.

[3] Clifford Geertz, *After the Fact: Two Countries, Four Decades, One Anthropologist* (Cambridge: Harvard University Press, 1995), 166.

61

Site, and I read history and biography in high school, hiding out in the stacks to read when I was working and should have been reshelving books at the Edwardsville Public Library where I had a job through high school.

I took an interest in history as an undergraduate at Illinois State University when one of my favorite professors in the Political Science Department gave me a copy of Russell Jacoby's *Social Amnesia: A Critique of Conformist Psychology from Adler to Laing*.[4] I was already interested in the critical theory and Marxist theory as an undergraduate, and Jacoby's work made a lasting impression on me in a time when I was reading works like Theodor Adorno and Max Horkheimer's *Dialectic of Enlightenment*, Herbert Marcuse's *One Dimensional Man*, and other works. I had immersed myself in reading critical theorists and Marxist theorists, in part, because of their careful attention to historical perspectives, so when I read Jacoby's *Social Amnesia*, it drew me to a much more historical approach of the study of political science, one that I still work with over thirty years later.

Mike Davis' *Prisoners of the American Dream: Politics and Economy in the History of the US Working Class* is another book I read as an undergraduate at Illinois State University, and it gave me a sprawling view of American politics, economics, and history, all through the lens of a Marxist perspective that I had been drawn to for many years.[5] I knew between Jacoby's *Social Amnesia* and Davis' *Prisoners of the American Dream* that whatever else I ended up studying, I would work with a historical perspective in the study of political science. I don't think any two books left as much of an impression on me from my time as an undergraduate as *Social Amnesia* and *Prisoners of the American Dream*, and I still reread them and recommend them to my own students almost thirty years later.

I arrived at the University of Wisconsin-Madison to start my doctoral studies in the Political Science Department, and I immersed myself not just in the Political Science Department, but in any number of departments and programs across that campus. I spent whatever spare time I had going to guest lectures and getting to know graduate students and faculty in departments across the Wisconsin campus. I took seminars in several departments, including Sociology, Environmental Studies, and Geography. I also took part in lectures and seminars in Wisconsin's History Department, and I formed friendships with graduate students in the History Department. I spent considerable time in the Wisconsin Historical Society and its vast collection of books, documents, and special collections.[6] I wrote most of my dissertation outline in the reading room of the Historical Society, and I researched the conservationist movement in the early twentieth century and postwar environmental organizations and groups as well as the civil rights movement.

---

[4] Russell Jacoby, *Social Amnesia: A Critique of Conformist Psychology from Adler to Laing* (Boston: Beacon Press, 1975).

[5] Mike Davis, *Prisoners of the American Dream: Politics and Economy in the History of the U.S. Working Class* (Brooklyn: Verso, 1986).

[6] I threw myself into reading almost anything I could get my hands on about the history of environmental activism and political movements more generally in American history. I spent the better part of a year's time in the Wisconsin Historical Society's stacks, reading everything I could get my hands on about twentieth century conservationist and preservationist movements. The Historical Society, across the street from the Memorial Union and its Terrace overlooking Lake Mendota, was the perfect setting for months of reading and sketching out my travel plans as I prepared to hit the road.

Figure 4.1 Wisconsin Historical Society

© EQRoy/Shutterstock.com

When I finally decided to write my dissertation on the intersections of race, ethnicity, class, and environmental pollution, I made every effort to look at the histories of the communities in Louisiana, New Mexico, and everywhere else that I spent time as part of my fieldwork. I like to think that the year or so I spent in the stacks and in the reading rooms of the Wisconsin Historical Society preparing for my fieldwork for my dissertation instilled in me even greater appreciation for incorporating a historical perspective into the research and work I do today as a political scientist. I traveled across the country from the backroads of Baton Rouge to the freeways of Los Angeles, learning as much as I could about the history of activism and politics in Louisiana, New Mexico, and elsewhere, and as I finished my travels to return to write and defend my doctoral dissertation back in Wisconsin, I was drawn in many ways in my thinking back to the South as a part of the country I hoped might spent more time and return to for a longer time.

I scarcely finished writing and defending my doctoral dissertation at the University of Wisconsin-Madison when that time arrived more quickly than I'd imagined, and I moved to coastal Georgia just outside of Savannah and began teaching at Georgia Southern University in Statesboro. I spent some time briefly in Georgia in my travels during my dissertation fieldwork, and I knew enough about the state's history before I moved here to know that I was in the right place to think about some of the things I had been starting to think about

Figure 4.2 Savannah, Georgia

© Sean Pavone/Shutterstock.com

during my graduate studies in Wisconsin. I felt at that time that I would continue to study the history of political movements in general and of the environmental justice movement, and I knew that Georgia presented itself as an obvious place to be able to study and work more closely with the kinds of organizations and groups I studied in my dissertation fieldwork. I felt I also would expand my study of the environmental justice movement that I had studied in Louisiana, New Mexico, and elsewhere in my doctoral fieldwork by studying and working with these same groups in Georgia, and I began to reach out almost immediately upon arriving in Statesboro to environmental justice activists in Savannah and in several other communities across South Georgia.

I spent almost two or three years of my teaching at Georgia Southern University still working with much of the research and writing I had done in my doctoral studies on the environmental justice movement, and I published several journal articles as well as my book, *Where We Live, Work and Play: The Environmental Justice Movement and the Struggle for a New Environmentalism.*[7]

---

[7] Patrick Novotny, *Where We Live, Work and Play: The Environmental Justice Movement and the Struggle for a New Environmentalism* (Westport, CT: Praeger, 2000).

I kept my interest in the environmental justice groups of the kind I studied in my dissertation fieldwork, but I saw my work take a turn much more to the study of American political institutions, including campaigning and political advertising, the press in American politics, political parties, and such. I lived in Savannah at the time, and I began what has been more than twenty years of interest and study of the history of that city and of Georgia's early history.

I also took an interest in the history of Georgia Southern University and several of its Presidents in the mid-twentieth century, Dr. Guy Wells and Dr. Marvin Pittman, an interest that eventually took me to a much larger project on the history of Georgia politics in the 1940s, *This Georgia Rising: Education, Civil Rights, and the Politics of Change in Georgia in the 1940s*.[8] Exploring the political history of Georgia in the twentieth century is something I still do as a part of my teaching and some of my research and writing, but recent work has led me to return to the history of American institutions, especially the history of the press in American politics and the history of the political parties in America. *The Press in American Politics, 1787–2012* is a book that I worked on over almost fifteen years of teaching at Georgia Southern University.[9] I talk about and teach and write regularly on both the press in American politics and political parties, and I anticipate continuing to do so for the remainder of my academic career. I explore the history of the arts and culture in American politics in some of the work I now do, including the role of films and motion pictures, the historical and political impact of television, the history of music in politics, and the arts and literature in twentieth century American politics. In these works, and in others, the historical perspective that I use in my work is foremost in almost everything that I study and in everything that I write.

I have lived in the South for more than twenty years, and I enjoy spending time learning more and reading on the history of the South, and of the South's part and place in the shaping of America's political institutions. I have been drawn to the study of history for almost the entire time of my work at Georgia Southern University, and I am as determined as I have ever been to keep a historical perspective in my work as a political scientist. I have spent time learning about and studying the civil rights movement in the South, and I have been fortunate to have visited some of the many historical sites of some of the key movements in the civil rights movement. I have learned a great deal of the history of Savannah where I spend a great deal of time, and I still learn more every time I read another book or learn more of the stories of that city's centuries-old history.[10] I still think from time-to-time

---

[8] Patrick Novotny, *This Georgia Rising: Education, Civil Rights, and the Politics of Change in Georgia in the 1940s* (Macon, GA: Mercer University Press, 2007).

[9] Patrick Novotny, *The Press in American Politics, 1787–2012* (Denver, CO: Praeger, 2014).

[10] I think one of the most important parts of the history I have studied in my twenty years living near Savannah is the history of work done by James Fallows and his twelve-member research staff on the environmental pollution of the Savannah River in the 1960s and the early 1970s. I was given a copy of *The Water Lords* shortly after arriving in Savannah, and I have read and reread it in the years since. Fallows' work and that of his staff, who lived in the Summer of 1970 in downtown Savannah, was published in 1971s *The Water Lords: Ralph Nader's Study Group Report on Industry and Environmental Crisis in Savannah, Georgia*. James M. Fallows, *The Water Lords: Ralph Nader's Study Group Report on Industry and Environmental Crisis in Savannah, Georgia* (New York: Grossman Publishers, 1971).

of returning to live in the Midwest, but I am likely to live here for some time to come, and I am still learning so much of the history of Georgia and of the South.

"The whole secret of politics is knowing who hates who," Kevin Phillips told Garry Wills, writing at the time his 1970 *Nixon Agonistes: The Crisis of the Self-Made Man*.[11] Phillips' county-by-county analysis of the history of voting and elections proved itself a strategic component of the Republican playbook in Tuesday, November 5, 1968s election of Richard Nixon, and Phillips' fine-grained history is the basis of the state-by-state analysis in the book he published shortly after Nixon won, Phillips' 1969 *The Emerging Republican Majority*.[12] Phillips, Wills tells us in his interview with the Republican strategist shortly after 1968s campaign, "[is] animated by one ambition—to know who hates who. 'That is the secret,' he says with a disarming boyish grin."[13] I think Phillips' secret-of-politics-is-knowing-who-hates-who and his election-by-election, state-by-state historical perspective is well-worth consideration by any serious student of politics, and I use it when I discuss thinking about politics in broadly definitional terms with my own students. I applaud what Phillips brings to the study of political science, and I tell my students that it is <u>only</u> when we study politics with a historical perspective that we can ever know why it is that these feelings are every bit as formidable as Phillips tells us they are. I think the only way to study and to know why these feelings are so formidable in our politics is for political scientists to study how these feelings are formed over time, and I believe the <u>only way</u> to study this is to study history.

I said in Chapter 1, and I say here in Chapter 4, that political scientists can and should always bring to bear the perspective of history to their studies of the present. Harold D. Lasswell's who gets what, when, how is a mostly static and a historical framework unless a historical viewpoint is brought to bear. Who has gotten what before now and how they have gotten it in the <u>past</u> is the only way we can ever understand who <u>gets</u> what, when, how <u>now</u>. I said in Chapter 1 that political scientists need to take a step back to look at the decisions made in the past. Studying how these decisions were made in the past, and studying the institutions that were a part of these decisions, is essential to our analysis and our thinking when we study decisions made in the present. I think any political scientist wanting to understand the decisions of the present is going to want to always look at the decisions that have been made in the past and how the decision-making institutions, personalities, and procedures have changed since then.

"There is nothing new in the world except the history you do not know," President Truman told author William Hillman in an interview during Truman's second term in the white House.[14] I regard Truman's words as some of the most relevant to the teaching and writing I do from a historical perspective. Truman's own love of history as a young man growing up in Missouri is a storied part of his biography.[15] The thirty-third President of the United States' lifetime of reading history shaped his own

---

[11] Garry Wills, *Nixon Agonistes: The Crisis of the Self-Made Man* (Boston: Houghton Mifflin, 1970), 265.

[12] Kevin P. Phillips, *The Emerging Republican Majority* (New Rochelle, NY: Arlington House, 1969).

[13] Wills, *Nixon Agonistes*, 265.

[14] William Hillman, *Mr. President: The First Publication from the Personal Diaries, Private Letters, Papers, and Revealing Interviews of Harry S. Truman, President of the United States of America* (New York: Farrar Straus and Young, 1952), 81.

[15] Independence's library, with its 2000 volumes at the time of Truman's childhood, is a focal point for this part of the President's life. "He grew dutifully, conspicuously studious, spending long afternoons in the town library, watched

Figure 4.3 Jackson County Courthouse, Independence, Missouri

© Joseph Sohm/Shutterstock.com

life and time in the White House as much as any President, and a centerpiece of the National Park Service (NPS) Harry S. Truman National Historic Site in Independence, Missouri is his private library in his home where he enjoyed years of reading after leaving the White House. His Presidency was met with some of the most consequential, far-reaching decisions of any President in the twentieth century, decisions undoubtedly influenced by Truman's own enthusiasm for his reading of history.

History is everything, and it is everywhere. It is a part of every place. It is in academic journals, and it is in bestselling biographies, books, and works of all kind. It is argued about,

over by a plaster bust of Ben Franklin," David McCullough tells us of a young Harry Truman. "Harry and Charlie Ross vowed to read all of them, encyclopedias included," McCullough tells us of the 2000 books in the Independence library that Truman and his childhood friend, Charlie Ross, claimed to have successfully read. "History," McCullough writes, "became a passion, as he worked his way through a shelf of standard works on ancient Egypt, Greece, and Rome. 'He had a real feeling for history,' [Truman's cousin Ethel Noland] said, 'that it wasn't something in a book, that it was part of life, a section of life or a former time, that it was of interest because it had to do with people.' He himself later said it was 'true facts' that he wanted. 'Reading history, to me, was far more than a romantic adventure. It was solid instruction and wise teaching which I somehow felt that I wanted and needed.'" David McCullough, *Truman* (New York: Simon and Schuster, 1992), 58.

Figure 4.4 National Archives, Washington, D.C.
© Orhan Cam/Shutterstock.com

disagreed upon, written about, and read by elected officials in debates of all kind at the highest levels, and it is the in work of genealogy and family histories, newsletters, and reunions. It is in classrooms, and it is in school libraries and in media centers. It is roadside markers maintained by state, county, and local historical societies, and it is the digitalization of documents, maps, photographs, and postcards in county courthouses, nonprofits, and libraries of all kinds. It is framed pictures or faded news clippings hanging on the walls of corner taverns and dive-bars, and it is the tourists in busses, in trolleys, and in walking tours of all kinds in their destinations and travels everywhere. It is the National Archives and Records Administration (NARA) and its fourteen Presidential libraries and museums. It is the National Archives Building on Pennsylvania Avenue NW just blocks from the Capitol and the White House. It is the Senate Historical Office, and it is the Office of the Historian and the Office of Art and Archives in the House of Representatives on Capitol Hill. It is NARA's National Historical Publications and Records Commission (NHPRC), and it is that commission's assistance in curating multivolume collections of the writings of John Adams by editors at the

Massachusetts Historical Society, of Benjamin Franklin's work by Yale University archivists, of Thomas Jefferson's writing at Princeton University, and of the writings of James Madison and George Washington by editors at the University of Virginia.

History is appreciated and attended to every day by the NPS, by historic sites and nonprofits of all kinds, and by museums and libraries visited every day by millions of people. It is archives, reading rooms, special collections, and microfilm records and collections of all kinds in state historical societies, public libraries, county courthouses, and other government buildings. It is the local history section of small bookstores and used bookstores, their shelves with books telling the local stories of families, businesses, and local pastimes. It is in C-SPAN specials and its C-SPAN2 BookTV interviews with authors of biography and histories of all kinds. It is commercial services for individuals looking to document and trace their family ancestry and lineages.

Figure 4.5 C-SPAN Video Library and Archives, Purdue University, West Lafayette, Indiana

© Jonathan Weiss/Shutterstock.com

Archaeologists, archivists, conservationists, and librarians tirelessly work every day to preserve and to protect the past. Antique dealers, collectors, genealogists, tour guides, and others are essential when it comes to preserving and protecting the artifacts and the places and the stories of the past. I think all of us appreciate from our visits to historic homes, sites, museums, and private and public collections of all kinds that it is the work of dedicated professionals together with volunteers that do the bulk of the work every day to preserve and protect the past. I think it is just as easy for each of us to appreciate, too, that it is just as easy to <u>lose</u> the past in the blink of an eye. History is deleted, destroyed, forgotten, lost, and obliterated every day, and the digital era is a time no less fraught for preservation of the past. Deleting and discarding irreplaceable digital documents and materials takes place in the click of a computer mouse. Upgrades of digital hardware and software obliterate records of all kinds all the time. History is lost every day in the boxes and cabinets of records discarded in dumpsters, or lost to indifference or negligence in archival preservation and storage.

I wrote in Chapters 2 and 3 of the hardwork and the self-discipline I feel is essential to both reading and writing, so I will stay with this and say here in Chapter 4 that I feel it is this same hardwork and self-discipline to let us study with a historical perspective, especially for many students in political science. I know most students are drawn to the study of political science by the immediacy of the issues that are daily debated in campaigns, in courtrooms, and in the policy-making process. I devote a substantial part of my day, as I said in Chapter 2, to the breaking stories and news that comes to my e-mail inbox from a variety of sources, especially newspapers like *The New York Times*, *The Los Angeles Times*, and *The Atlanta Journal Constitution*, not to mention the many Google News

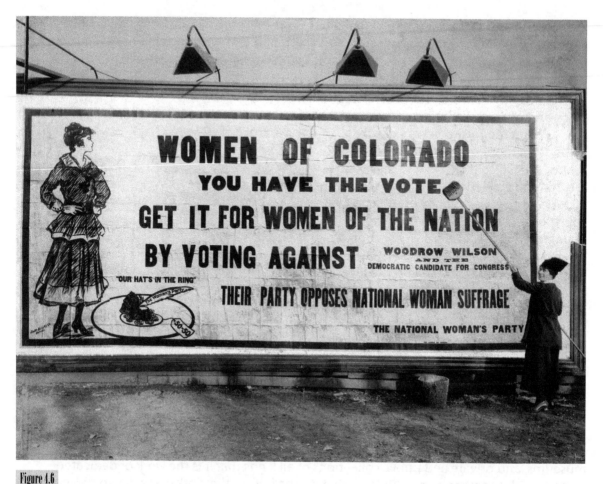

Figure 4.6

© Everett Historical/Shutterstock.com

Alerts that ping in my phone's e-mail at all hours of the day. I tell my students that the most exciting part of teaching in the field of political science are those headlines in the morning paper or breaking stories coming across the wire only hours or even minutes earlier that end up becoming examples or topics of discussion I use in that same day's classroom lectures.

I work with historical documents, books, and materials of all kinds when it comes to much of the writing I do, and I believe that the historical work I do offers a depth of perspective to the headlines and the stories that I read every day. When a historical perspective is brought to the analysis done by political scientists, I believe it helps to better explain the institutions and the personalities behind these headlines. I know that this kind of approach to the study of the politics, one that balances the here-and-now with serious work to connect with a wider historical perspective and point of view, is an approach that demands twice as much work if not more. History is a patience-demanding, time-consuming undertaking, so any political scientist wanting to bring this historical perspective to their analysis of the head-lines and stories of the day need to be prepared to do extensive reading, to be ready to work with books and materials that may sometimes be difficult to locate, and to travel to archives to access some materials. Long hours can be the cost for the long view that history affords us in the work we do.

I said in Chapter 1, and I will say here again in Chapter 4 that I feel it is always important for us to work with historical documents and materials in as original a format as available to us. For political scientists, when we work with a historical perspective, I think it is important to recognize that rarely if ever will we work with original archival materials or documents. With little if any training in handling archival materials or documents, it is unlikely that a political scientist will ever look at rare documents or archival materials firsthand. Archival collections require expertise and training in the care and handling of these documents, so what we as political scientists will almost always do is work with facsimiles of the archival material assembled, curated, and edited in volumes by historians and preservationists.

I work almost every day with books, with digitalized, online newspapers, with digitalized, scanned materials through Google Books, with digitalized newspapers from archives on newspaper Websites and from LexisNexis Academic, and scholarly journals through data-bases including Google Scholar, JSTOR, and others. I am always attentive to walking back through whatever sources I use to find as original and as primary a reference as I can for whatever I am looking at. If I have a quote, I want to follow the trail through books or other works to find the original citation or as early a source-of-record I can find for these words.[16] As I said in Chapter 1, instead of quoting a scholarly work that quotes a figure or person in the past, I feel it is important that I take the time to come as close as I can to finding these words in their original sources. If I find a quote from a historic figure of interest, I immediately search through these digitalized databases and others until I find it in the earliest or the most original source I can. Sometimes, it might be in a first edition of a book, or other times, it may be tracking a scholar's words through several different editions or in different publications until I can find their earliest or their first use of the words I am studying.

When I work with historical documents such as correspondence or letters by some of the early figures in the history of early American politics, to cite one example, I prefer to cite

---

[16] I do a considerable amount of my own work following up on quotations, and much of that I do to find as early and as original a source as I can when citing the words of public figures or authors. If I find a more recent quotation less than, say, forty years old, I will enter it into LexisNexis Academic or other databases. For earlier quotations, Google Books, Google Scholar, or JSTOR are usually where I will begin. I like to use quotations to track down other scholarly articles or works. It sometimes allows me to find books or book chapters, especially older, often out-of-print books that can provide additional insights. When I write and cite a footnote, I almost always want to cite the *hardback* edition rather than the paperback, since it is almost always the hardback that will be in most library stacks if a reader wants to look up the footnote themselves. I obviously want to make sure to cite the edition if it is a first or second or later edition, but citing the hardback is a small way of making sure that readers are more likely to be able to find materials when there are page-numbering differences between the hardback and paperback editions.

their correspondence or writings from the multivolume collections published by Princeton University Press, the University of Virginia Press, and others. Still other multivolume collections, like the *Documentary History of the First Federal Congress, 1789–1791*, a twenty-volume series under the direction of Charlene Bangs Bickford and her colleagues and published by the Johns Hopkins University Press, or Columbia University Press' *The Documentary History of the Supreme Court of the United States, 1789–1800*, a multivolume series curated and edited by Maeva Marcus and her colleagues with the Supreme Court Historical Society's Documentary History Project, offer a remarkable source of material. I think it is useful for scholars and students to take the time to find the specific page or pages in volumes such as these, to read whatever it is in its entirety to appreciate the fullness of this writing, and then to cite from these volumes in their own references or footnotes.

I find that biographies, annotated and edited volumes like those of NARA's NHPRC, and the like are some of the best sources of historical documentation I use as a political scientist, and I use books, biographies, and whatever historical materials I can find when I research and write much of the work that I do. I find, also, that of all the historical documents and primary source materials that I read and that I reference in my writing, I am most at ease in the use of newspapers in writing much of the work that I do. I use newspapers in almost every published work that I do, and I find newspapers to be some of the easiest-to-use and most effective material of any that I work with when I work with more historical topics. I find that newspapers are one of the most important primary documents that I use when I bring a historical perspective to bear in the work that I do. I take seriously the words of the late Philip L. Graham, who called newspapers the first rough draft of history, as I discussed in Chapter 3. Every time I am in Washington, DC and I spend time in the Newseum on Pennsylvania Avenue NW, I am always struck by the truth of this idea when I see these words of Graham inscribed in the very walls of the fifth floor of that magnificent museum.

"For period flavor," Barbara W. Tuchman says, "newspapers are unsurpassed," describing newspapers and their page after page of details of the stories of the day as useful for evoking the feel of the time as much as the facts of the day. "As to newspapers, I like them for period flavor perhaps more than for factual information," Tuchman says.[17] I completely agree with Tuchman's apt description of newspapers as offering the feel and the flavor of the past as much as the facts of the day, and I, like Tuchman, turn to the pages of newspapers as almost always the first place I turn for the details and the fine-grain richness that I like to include in my writing.

I know that referencing and researching much of what I write with newspapers tends to make almost everything I write that much more descriptive when I am writing the stories of the political past. Newspapers are one of the first and most important sources of primary documentation in the work that I do, and I feel that their reporting, especially in papers in the nineteenth century and in the beginning and middle of the twentieth century, is a trea-sure trove for political scientists. At the turn of the century and well into the mid-twentieth century, most cities and towns had competing daily papers. In cities with separately-owned daily papers, their competition for readership and circulation usually meant that their report-ing of stories and the depth and quality of their journalism was of a standard that still holds up exceptionally well to this day. To read a newspaper in the late nineteenth or the early and mid-twentieth century is to see page after page and column after column in these papers, day after day, filled with sometimes dozens of stories and short items on each page, all mate-rial that can enrich our writing.

With the rise of commercial broadcast television in the years after the World War II and then especially cable television in the years of the 1970s and into the last decades of the twentieth century, the typical newspaper with their multiple short items and a dozen or more stories on each page steadily shifted toward a format of longer form reporting that made newspapers in some respects in the last forty or fifty years less the trove of stories for historians that they might have been a century ago in most instances. Twenty-first century digital transformations in infor-mation and news now have effectively eclipsed most print-newspapers today as papers struggle daily with their circulation, readership, and subscribership.

I use digitalized, online historic newspapers in almost everything that I write in my work, and I am accustomed now to be able to multiple-reference newspaper reporting and stories

---

[17] Barbara W. Tuchman, *Practicing History: Selected Essays by Barbara W. Tuchman* (New York: Alfred A. Knopf, 1981), 42.

Figure 4.8

© Y Photo Studio/Shutterstock.com

across several of the digitalized, online historic newspaper platforms that I have immediate access to and use regularly. *The New York Times'* Times Machine, *The Chicago Tribune* Archives, ProQuest Historical Newspapers including *The Atlanta Constitution*, and other digitalized, online historic newspapers are some of the services I use on a regular basis when I write much of the writing I do from a historical perspective. I am grateful for the easily-searchable, online accessibility that is brought to my desktop and to my computer through databases like ProQuest Historical Newspapers as well as digitalized archival services from newspapers themselves, and even services like Google News Archive. EBSCOhost Newspaper Source and LexisNexis Academic offer still more options for digitally accessible historical papers, but as with ProQuest Historical Newspapers, whenever there is a newspaper story that is not available as a full-page image but still important enough for me to reference in my research, I often will request the microfilm reels through interlibrary loan services, and I will take the time for these to arrive for me to reference and use through the microfilm readers. I like to be able to cite the page number and have the full reference for stories in papers, especially multipage stories, so having the full-page images means manual microfilm is still the only option for those papers not yet digitally available.

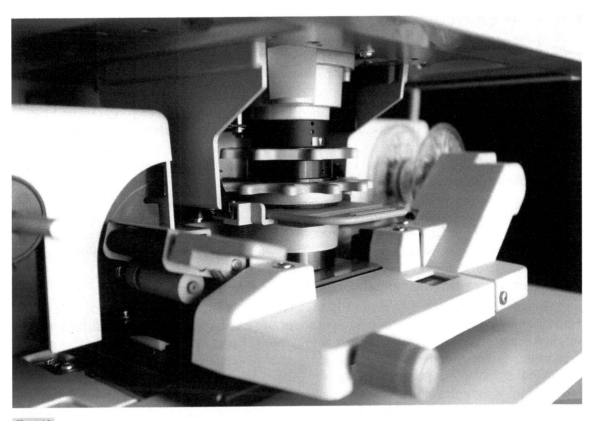

I recall the years from my doctoral studies at the University of Wisconsin-Madison through my early years as a faculty member at Georgia Southern University working with microfilm reader machines and spooling reel-after-reel of plastic film through the spinning-spools and the glass-and-metal plates on these machines. I was accustomed to taking the time almost every day to walk to the library, find the right cartons of microfilm, thread it on the spools of the microfilm reader, and then crank the microfilm forward and backward until I finally found the right dates and pages and stories on these pages. Now, from *The New York Times'* Times Machine to *The Chicago Tribune* Archives to ProQuest Historical Newspapers and other sites I use almost every day, I can bring these materials directly to my desktop and, as importantly, I can <u>multiple-source</u> coverage for the <u>same events</u> on the <u>same days</u> across several different papers within a matter of minutes to compare coverage and reporting.

I tell my students that when they work with newspapers in their own research, whether it is on a microfilm reader machine or digitalized, online sites like *The New York Times'* Times Machine or ProQuest Historical Newspapers, or any others, they always need <u>to look at the whole page</u>, to look for the unexpected stories and to scan the full pages for any headlines that might be useful in that moment, or that can be copied and set aside for potential future projects. I say to my students that they need to look at <u>everything</u> on the page—including the weather—to make sure they have the <u>feel</u> for the time and the place and not just the news item they are looking for.[18] I tell my students how important I believe it is for them to cross-reference and multiple-source news stories for the same events on the same days in several different papers, something now done with the click-of-a-mouse convenience in seconds thanks to multipaper, online, digitalized archives like ProQuest Historical Newspapers.

I will talk a great deal about the importance of getting out and traveling and seeing things ourselves in Chapter 5, and I will take just a moment here to reflect on the relationship that I think is important between the historical perspective I incorporate into my work and the travel I do and that I think that other political scientists should do in the work we do. I travel whenever I have the opportunity, and I am eager always when the opportunity to travel arises to spend time before my trip, sometimes weeks or longer, looking for any historical readings I can find to help me better understand where I am traveling. I read histories of the places I visit before my travels to take advantage of my time there, and so I can know more than just the historical-marker descriptions of the locations or sites of interest I see while I am there. I like to spend time, both before I travel to a destination, while I am there at that destination, and even when I return from there, to learn more and read more about these places, especially their histories.

I am interested in the writing of those historians and authors of biographies and other books who take the time to visit the places they write about and where the figures they write about in history lived, spent their time, and worked in their lifetimes. I respect figures like David McCullough and his travels to places like Independence, Missouri in his writing on the life of President Harry Truman. I applaud the time he's spent on North Carolina's Outer Banks in writing his magnificent, must-read history of the Wright brothers.[19] I admire Robert Caro and his writing on the life of President Lyndon Johnson, as Caro has spent time in the Texas countryside that Johnson called home to better understand the life of Johnson and his legacy. He and his wife, Ina, spent considerable time over the years in Texas, living in Texas for almost three years talking with family and friends of the late President, looking through papers at the Lyndon Baines Johnson Library and Museum in Austin, and, most importantly, exploring and getting the feel of the land in the Hill Country and the places where Johnson and his family made their home.

"'You've got to get out of the library' and talk to real people," Caro says, a writer with a legendary willingness to get away from the desk and out of the office and to the places where people live and where history was made and is made.[20] I couldn't agree more with Caro, and I think it is essential for us to go to the places we write about whenever it is possible, and to stay there for however long it takes to get the atmosphere and the feel of a place right in the words we write. When I finished writing this chapter, Caro announced his plans

---

[18] I should say that it is also about looking at other pages in these newspapers, not just the page with the news item being studied. *Browsing* through the pages of digitally-archived historic newspapers in services like ProQuest Historical Newspapers or turning the pages on the spool of archived microfilm if using a microfilm reader to look on additional pages as available for any additional news items on your topic or even on unrelated items of possible interest to other projects is something I encourage for my students.

[19] David McCullough, *The Wright Brothers* (New York: Simon and Schuster, 2015), 336.

[20] Nicholas Von Hoffman, "Robert Caro's Holy Fire." *Vanity Fair* 53, no. 4 (April 1990): 218.

Figure 4.10   Lyndon B. Johnson National Historical Park, Stonewall, Texas

© Mike Brake/Shutterstock.com

for his long-anticipated travels to Vietnam as a part of the completion of his fifth volume on the life of President Lyndon Johnson.[21] I admire the work of Caro to visit the places he writes about, and I have cited it throughout this book for that very reason, among others. I regard his attention-to-detail, and his skills as an interviewer and observer to be some of the best of any historian or writer that I know, and I am grateful for the time he spent in New York City's East Tremont neighborhood and others just prior to some of the evictions of its residents, his time spent in Texas' Hill Country, and the time on Capitol Hill in Washington, DC as an exemplar for any authors wanting to write detailed descriptions of the places they write about.[22] I admire and applaud his getting out to talk with people when he writes about places, his eagerness to travel and to spend time taking in these places, and I appreciate his announced plans to travel to Vietnam as a part of completing his work on Lyndon Johnson, travels that will give him the perspective of the Vietnamese who lived, died, and fought in that war.

---

[21] John Willliams, "Robert Caro Nears End of Research on L.B.J." *The New York Times* Saturday, June 3, 2017, C3.

[22] Robert Caro, "The Art of Biography." *The Paris Review* 216 (Spring 2016): 160.

I see history as something that is in everything around us, and I think it is done best by taking everything in around us. I like to talk with people about the history I read about and study, and I like to hear from them about the history they know, and I like to listen to the stories they tell. Experiencing a place for yourself, immersing yourself there, and living there for how-ever long it takes to make sense of it and to get an idea of the place, is what I will talk about in Chapter 5. I think political scientists can learn from historians like Caro, McCullough, Tuchman, and others who do this in their research and in their writing.

William E. Leuchtenburg's *American Places: Encounters with History* is a remarkable volume I recommend to anyone with an interest in history, and I especially like it because it makes this connection between writing on history and the time spent by writers in these places to pick up from and learn more about the places themselves. In his work, Leuchtenburg brings together a group of talented historians who have spent time travel-ing to and even living in the places they have written about in their works. Leuchtenburg's collection is an illustration of the value that I find in my own work in spending time when visiting these locations. I like to get outside and walk the streets, and I like to spend time looking not just at the more popular historic locations and settings. I also like to read about and find those more out-of-the-way places to visit that are somewhat off the beaten path. Leuchtenburg, along with historians and biographers in his collection, certainly know the value of visiting the places that shaped the lives of those figures they write about, and I agree completely with them that the time spent exploring and visiting a place firsthand gives us that much more detail and descriptive insight when we go to tell the story and write it up.

In Chapter 1, I made the case for the importance of <u>location</u> to the study of political science, and I will return to this in Chapters 5 and 6. I would say here in Chapter 4 that a connection with the places and locations we research and study and write about is important, whether it is the work of political scientists or it is the work of historians writing about events that took place many years earlier. Whether it is a political scientist walking the hallways and spending time in their work on Capitol Hill in Washington, DC, or it is a historian taking the time to walk across the fields in Northern France studying the World War I so they might get a feel for the physical landscape, I feel it is important to be a part of the places we study and write about. Walking the hallways on Capitol Hill as McCullough did to understand the sounds of the footsteps as Harry Truman rushed through its hallways in April 1945 upon learning of the death of Franklin Roosevelt, or walking some of these same hallways as Caro did to get a feel for the offices where Lyndon Johnson spent his time in the House and then Senate, or Tuchman's driving across the countryside in Belgium, Luxembourg, and Northern France as a part of her Pulitzer Prize-winning 1962 *The Guns of August*, I think the writing of historians and the writing of political scientists is enlivened and is enriched by the firsthand time spent in these places.

I respect the writing of Tuchman as much as almost any historian who writes on the writing of history, and I recommend her work to colleagues and students who are working with their own writing. I said in Chapter 3 that Tuchman's advice on writing is some of the most insightful that I know, and I often tell my students her advice to writers on accuracy and attention-to-detail in their writing is something to be taken to heart. Writing is the heart of history, Tuchman tells us. "I am a writer first whose subject is history," Tuchman says in 1981s *Practicing History: Selected Essays*.[23] It is the work of the historian to commit to connecting with their readers, mostly through the careful selection of the stories they tell as well as consideration of the meanings and the motives that move history.

"I do not invent anything, even the weather," Tuchman tells us in 1981's *Practicing History: Selected Essays*.[24] I am always struck by the sincerity of Tuchman's insistence on avoiding embellishment in her writing, and I talk with and teach this to my students to remind them of how important it is to tell authentic story with accurate attention-to-detail. I also admire how Tuchman emphasizes traveling to "get the feeling" of the place, as Tuchman tells her readers, travels and visits that "[are] productive of insights." "There is nothing like research on the spot," Tuchman says, traveling to the places she writes about.[25] Tuchman tells us of the importance of visiting the places she writes about, something I completely agree when it comes to the work

---

[23] Barbara W. Tuchman, *Practicing History: Selected Essays by Barbara W. Tuchman* (New York: Alfred A. Knopf, 1981), 69.
[24] Ibid., 18.
[25] Ibid., 69.

of historians, political scientists, and any writer wanting to tell the story of a place.[26] "As a source of understanding, nothing is more valuable than knowing the scene in person," Tuchman tells us.[27] She tells us of the time spent in archives and in libraries, even talking about her encounters with some of her fellow library patrons in one of her favorite places to write, the New York Public Library (NYPL) Reading Room on Fifth Avenue, and in other archives and libraries.[28] "To roam the stacks is of course the most delightful, if not the most disciplined, form of research, and the most productive of discoveries," Tuchman says, yet it is less the long hours in the stacks turning the pages in the archives than it is the hardwork ("much harder and takes twice as long") of writing it all waiting back at their desks.[29] We look at documents, we spend time in archives, we turn the pages, we take notes, we travel, we talk with people, but mostly we write.

I wholeheartedly agree with Tuchman when she describes the enjoyment of the research we do in libraries when we assemble our historical materials. I can't think of any part of the work that I do in my research and my writing that I enjoy more than the hours I spend in libraries pulling books off the shelves, looking at the titles on either side of the books on the shelves I am there to look at, taking these stacks of books to nearby tables or sometimes sitting cross-legged right there in the aisle of the stacks to look through the books. As I mentioned in Chapter 2, I am never in a library without pens, paper, and my phone, taking photographs of pages to use

---

[26] Tuchman tells readers of her time spent traveling to some of the various locations for interviews, never using a tape recorder ("I can't imagine myself plunking a machine down in front of someone and saying, 'Now, talk'"), and of visiting archives and libraries, but I think the most important is what she describes in several different places in 1981s *Practicing History* as "research on the spot," including a discussion on her most famous book, *The Guns of August*:

> Even more immediate is research on the spot. Before writing *The Guns* I rented a little Renault and in another August drove over the battle areas of August 1914, following the track of the German invasion through Luxembourg, Belgium, and northern France. Besides obtaining a feeling of the geography, distances, and terrain involved in military movements, I saw the fields ripe with grain which the cavalry would have trampled, measured the great width of the Meuse at Liege, and saw how the lost territory of Alsace looked to the French soldiers who gazed down upon it from the heights of the Vosges. I learned the discomfort of the Belgian *pave* and discovered, in the course of losing my way almost permanently in a tangle of country roads in a hunt for the house that had been British Headquarters, why a British motorcycle dispatch rider in 1914 had taken three hours to cover twenty-five miles. Clearly, owing to the British officers' preference for country houses, he had not been able to find Headquarters either. French army commanders, I noticed, located themselves in *towns*, with railroad stations and telegraph offices.

Tuchman's account of her time spent in Belgium, Luxembourg, and elsewhere in researching and writing 1962s *The Guns of August* is only one of the stories of her "research on the spot" she tells in *Practicing History*. Tuchman, *Practicing History*, 20, Italics in Original.

[27] Tuchman, *Practicing History*, 61.

[28] "Some come in out of the cold, others to pursue often strange devices," Tuchman says of some of the other patrons in the NYPL Reading Room at 476, fifth Avenue. "Once," Tuchman recounts, "a lady sat across from me with a large cloth bag from which she extracted a variety of embossed paper napkins, colored pencils with which she decorated the napkins, envelopes into which she stuffed them, an address book which she fiercely leafed for names to write on the envelopes, stamps, and a sponge to finish the process." Tuchman, *Practicing History*, 78.

[29] Ibid.

Figure 4.12 New York Public Library (NYPL) Reading Room, Fifth Avenue, New York City

© travelview/Shutterstock.com

later in my referencing and my writing and sending e-mails to myself or updating Google Docs. Taking those stacks of books to a nearby table and leafing through their pages and looking for the material that I am trying to find to reference in my writing is some of my most enjoyable work that I do, and I completely agree with Tuchman that it can be so enjoyable to pull these books from the shelves and leaf through them that it is easy to forget that our work of writing is what awaits.[30] We must step out of the stacks and sit down at the desk, and do the writing that is the most important work in history.

I have a great appreciation and interest in the historical perspective in almost all the writing that I do, and I like to go as far back in my history as I can in my writing. I like to trace some of the historical perspectives I write about in my work as far back as I can go, even if it something that I may well end up <u>not</u> using in the final published work that I do. As I said in Chapter 3, I experience this myself in some of the writing I do where a historical perspective is a part. In *The Press in American Politics, 1787–2012*, I spent many weeks reading and researching and writing about the earliest days of printing presses in the North American colonies in the early 1600s. I traced in considerable detail the shipment of printing presses from London to Cambridge, Massachusetts, and then to Boston, Philadelphia, and elsewhere, all under the watchful eye of colonial authorities and

---

[30] Ibid., 79.

Royal Governors. I became fascinated with the technology itself of printing press, and learned a great deal, more than I ever believed I would, about the presses, their operation, the print shops where they operated, and most of all the printers. I traced this early generation of printing path-breakers to the era of Benjamin Franklin and others who were a part of printing's second century in North America, and their struggles in the years prior to the War of Independence.

I read and researched and wrote for months on the printers and their print shops from the 1630s through the 1770s and after, yet I made the decision after careful thought to begin *The Press in American Politics, 1787–2012* at the time of the Constitutional Convention. I was disappointed in one sense that this writing, two fully-completed chapters, did not make it in the published book, but I was not disappointed in any way given the knowledge I learned of this era in history. I learned more than I ever thought I would on this era in the history of America in the colonial era and in the War of Independence, and I am still curious and continue to do some reading in this era from time to time, even though I did not publish it in *The Press in American Politics, 1787–2014*.

I had much the same experience in writing *The Press in American Politics, 1787–2012* when writing about printers and their newspapers in the 1790s and the early 1800s, when some began to make the journey into the territories in places like Illinois, Indiana, Missouri, and elsewhere. I grew curious about some of the stories of the printers who hauled their presses, ink, paper, and other supplies across some of the barely-passable roads and trails of the Western regions of the country at that time, navigating rivers and streams, and settling in barely-settled towns. I even visited the fields along the Mississippi River near the Southern Illinois town of Kaskaskia where the once-thriving first territorial capital of Illinois was settled, and where the first printer in the state, Matthew Duncan, set up the first print shop and printed the first paper, *The Illinois Herald*, in the territory. In the end, some of this research and work did make it into the writing I published in *The Press in American Politics, 1787–2014*, but much more of the work and writing I did ended up as pages on my office floor, cut as I made the hard choices of what to make space for and leave in the final published book. As with the work I did on printing in the 1630s until the War of Independence, I still benefitted immensely from doing this research, and it ignited a great curiosity that I am still interested in.

I like the <u>tactile</u> part of working with history as much as I appreciate the breadth and the depth that historical perspectives bring to my work as a political scientist. I enjoy walking to the library, and pulling books off the shelves in the Library of Congress D or E or F sections, finding a place by the windows, and paging through them until I find the material I am looking for. I enjoy the hands-on feeling of paging through a book of history or a work of biography. I appreciate in every sense the words I quoted in Chapter 1 of Justice Oliver Wendell Holmes, Jr., who said "a page of history is worth a volume of logic."[31] I like the feel of looking at old documents, especially when I can work with old newspapers not just on the black-and-white plastic of microfilm or in

---

[31] *New York Trust Company et al., as Executors of Purdy v. Eisner*, Error to the District Court of the United States for the Southern District of New York, No. 286, Argued April 25, 26, 1921, Decided May 16, 1921. *United States Reports, Volume 256, Cases Adjudged in the Supreme Court at October Term, 1920, from April 11, 1921 to June 6, 1921.* The Banks Law Publishing Company, 1922, 349.

an online, digitalized format, but when I can page through an old newspaper by hand. I like getting lost in what I am looking at in the books, documents, old photographs, and other materials I read and study in libraries, the feeling of walking and working in the stacks ("To roam the stacks is of course the most delightful," as Tuchman says) and turning the pages of whatever documents or books or materials I am looking at there. I enjoy the feeling of learning something <u>new</u> about something that is <u>old</u> that I get whenever I get lost in the pages of histories and works of biography. I like the task of ferreting out some of the more interesting and important stories of the political past in old books, newspapers, or magazines, and especially looking at old photographs and maps and the like, and I like to look for history in out-of-the-way ways.

"There is nothing new in the world except the history you do not know," President Harry Truman said, as I wrote earlier in Chapter 4. I return to these words again and again in my thinking and my teaching and my writing when it comes to the historical perspective I bring to the work I do as a political scientist. I know of no words more apt to the writing I do with a historical perspective, and I think that all political scientists should do whatever they need to do to bring whatever historical perspective they can in their writing when it can help better explain topics to their readers. I like to learn something new about the past every day if I can, and I like to think it is discovering something new about something old that is always what keeps me turning pages and that is always what keeps me writing pages of my own.

CHAPTER
5

You Got Tuh *Go* There Tuh *Know* There

"When in Rome, do as you done in Milledgeville," the Georgia novelist Flannery O'Connor said in a letter to her friend, playwright Maryat Lee, in May 1957.[1] I opened Chapter 4 with the words of William Faulkner and Eugene O'Neill, so it is only fitting to open Chapter 5, whose title is from Zora Neale Hurston's 1939 novel *Their Eyes Were Watching God*, with the words of O'Connor. From Georgia's onetime capital with its Old Capitol Building, its Old Governor's Mansion, and the Central State Hospital that once filled many a Georgia child's nightmares, the Savannah-born O'Connor penned words we might well-consider some sixty years later.

I travel whenever I can, and I enjoy traveling as often as I can. I travel to enjoy the scenery and the sense of surprise of seeing new places, and I always like to relate the writing I do in some way with my travels to the places that I enjoy visiting with family and with friends. I like the sights, the sounds, and the sense of being away from my desk and away from my daily routine that I get when I travel. I was raised by parents who love to travel, and I had a sense of appreciation when I was young of the vastness of the United States as we drove coast-to-coast and took in the scenery as well as the history from our visits to any number of historical locations and sites of all kind. I remember from those travels our many visits to parks and sites with the National Park Service (NPS), and I still feel a great sense of appreciation and gratitude for these visits with my parents whenever I visit a NPS park or site today.

I enjoyed traveling when I was young, and as I grew older and took up a love of reading, I was drawn to novelists and writers whose works in some respects shared a common thread of travel as well. I grew up in Southern Illinois near the Mississippi River, and I loved reading everything I could about the river and its history. I read and reread Mark Twain's *Life on the Mississippi*, and I always enjoyed reading everything I could get my hands on about the river and its towns and cities like my hometown of St. Louis as well as Memphis, New Orleans, and others. I discovered the writings of Lawrence Ferlinghetti, Allen Ginsberg, and Jack Kerouac, and I read and reread many of their works, especially Kerouac's *On the Road* and *The Dharma*

---

[1] Flannery O'Connor writing in letter to Maryat Lee, Sunday, May 19, 1957, in *The Habit of Being: Letters of Flannery O'Connor, Selected and Edited by Sally Fitzgerald* (New York: Farrar, Straus and Giroux, 1979), 220.

Figure 5.1   City Lights Bookstore, San Francisco, California

© Steve Wood/Shutterstock.com

Bums.[2] Ferlinghetti's City Lights Bookstore in San Francisco is one of my favorite places to visit in one of my favorite cities in the United States, and I still reread Kerouac's *The Dharma Bums* as one of the books I take with me as a part of my reading whenever I travel on vacation for a longer time. I also fell under the spell of the late Hunter S. Thompson, and still own the same paperback copies I read and reread years ago of his *Fear and Loathing in Las Vegas* and *Fear and Loathing on the Campaign Trail 72* when I was in high school.

I spent many months as a part of the research for my doctoral dissertation traveling across the country, and I had some incredible experiences in my travels. I knew all the places that I wanted to visit, and I knew most of the questions I wanted to ask when I set out for my first of several research trips. I knew once I started logging miles behind the wheel, I would come up

---

[2] A lifetime possession I've kept near my desk from my days as an undergraduate political science major at Illinois State University through the present on my office bulletin board is a photograph of Jack Kerouac in New York City taken by Allen Ginsberg, Ginsberg inscribed on the photograph, sometime around September 1953. Kerouac is standing on the third floor fire-escape outside of Ginsberg's apartment with what Ginsberg captioned as a "railroad brakeman's rule book" in his jacket's pocket, a photograph today in the collection of one of my favorite museums, the National Gallery of Art in Washington, DC.

with new questions the longer I spent time on the road and the longer I stayed in these places. I knew that there were many questions I still didn't know even after a year of sitting and studying in the library back at the University of Wisconsin-Madison, and I knew I had to spend time taking everything in before I would know the right questions to ask.

I spent months traveling and watching the work of neighborhood groups and local organizers in Albuquerque, in Los Angeles, in Baton Rouge, and in New Orleans as they worked to educate and to organize their communities to fight against the threats of environmental pollution from nearby industries. Union local members, housing advocates, and neighborhood associations were my entry point into these communities, and I spent days in offices or traveling with their members to meetings or local forums. The longer I spent someplace, the better idea I had of the questions that were most useful to ask. Evenings and weekends were mostly the time that I got to know these places better, and I sometimes was lucky to find that some of the people I met along the way were willing to take time in their spare time on these evenings or during these weekends to show me around their communities.

I had late-night meals in Baton Rouge where the cooking didn't begin until after midnight, and the meals and conversations stretched late into the night. I walked in the fields and saw family burial plots and small cemeteries in the shadow of chemical plants in Louisiana near the banks of the Mississippi River, and I talked with residents whose families lived on the land for generations and now lived with the threat of pollution. I walked through the debris of abandoned buildings and warehouses in Chicago and Milwaukee with local activists who showed me where homeless women and men had slept on cardboard right atop discarded chemicals and toxic materials. I spent weeks in Detroit and saw the desolation of neighborhoods compounded by environmental contamination. I explored the neighborhoods of New Orleans with residents fighting for healthier housing and living spaces for themselves, their children, and their neighbors. I rode some back roads in Louisiana with chemical plant workers in their pickup trucks in late-night drives to see some of the round-the-clock work of these plants.

I slept in my car a few nights, and I slept on back porches or couches, and I stayed in some of the dingiest motels I could imagine, motels that I seemed to have a knack for finding and that always were priced almost perfectly fit my bootstraps budget. I lived for a time in a house near the French Quarter, and had a cast of characters in some of the fellow-boarders in that house that might have made for a novel. I got to know the drive back-and-forth from New Orleans to Baton Rouge like it was the back of my hand. I got lost driving to meet people in their homes for interviews more times than I can remember, and I traveled without the conveniences of a cell phone, GPS, or even a decent map for some of these visits. I ate more takeout food from fast-food restaurants and drive-through windows than I ever should have in my travels. I lugged my typewriter everywhere I stayed, and I spent most evenings typing up my notes from my day's interviews or meetings. I prepared and planned to use a tape recorder for interviews, and I scrapped these plans almost immediately after the first several interviews that I did, realizing that I would get so much more out of taking notes by hand, learning how to listen for key points in the interviews, and then taking the time right away after these interviews to type up the material from them in sometimes pages of notes.

I learned a great deal about these communities, and about the struggles they confronted in connecting the economic and environmental threats that they faced in their communities. When I returned to the University of Wisconsin-Madison to write up my work in my dissertation in the last year of my graduate studies, I knew that I could never fully do justice to the women and men whose lives I had gotten to know for a time, but I knew that my years of work in libraries and seminar rooms had been worth it to have this chance to see parts of the country I might never have seen and to take the time to learn from, listen to, and even live for a time with people there in a way I never would quite be able to ever do again in my career. I finished my dissertation and defended it with a feeling of exhaustion and exhilaration as all PhD candidates can appreciate, yet I knew that in addition to the relief I felt from completing my dissertation, I'd seen some incredible parts of the country and I'd met and gotten to know some incredible people along the way. I knew that this idea of taking the time to travel, even if it just to the other side of town, is something well worth our time and our consideration as political scientists.

"It's uh known fact, Pheoby, you got tuh *go* there tuh *know* there," Hurston's character Janie Starks says in the closing pages of her 1937 *Their Eyes Were Watching God: A Novel.* "Yo' papa and yo' mama and nobody else can't tell yuh and show yuh," Starks says to the one of the novel's other characters, Pheoby Watson.[3] Hurston's acclaimed novel, published in its first edition by J.B. Lippincott Company in September 1937, was written while she was on a Guggenheim Fellowship in Haiti studying folk religions of the descendants of West African slaves. Hurston's insights and her ear for the stories and the traditions she studied in the South and in the West Indies and elsewhere made for a finely told storytelling on the pages of her novels and stories.

I think there is a lot to be said for the adage that you could fill a book with all the things that can't be learned in books. I know from my own experience the value of the face-to-face, firsthand, find-out-on-your-own approach to the study of politics that I will explore here in Chapter 5. I will take the time to explore this idea of getting out, getting into the mix, and getting as close to the source as we can when it comes to learning about politics, whether it is watching and working in the marbled corridors of a legislative setting like Capitol Hill in Washington, DC or in the remote corners of a town or village somewhere in halfway around the world. Libraries like the Wisconsin Historical Society where I spent almost a year of my doctoral studies outlining and sketching my dissertation are an important part of our research, but I feel that there comes a time in almost every project where we need to push aside our books and take that leap of faith into the world to see our ideas put to the test or given a chance to unfold in front of us. Setting forth on these travels as a part of our research is in some ways a profound expression of humility, a recognition that we don't know all the answers, that we don't know what we are going to find until we get there, and that all the reading and preparation and methodological training we have may mean very little when our frameworks and thinking through the issues we want to study come face-to-face with the realities of the people and the places we study.

---

[3] Zora Neale Hurston, *Their Eyes Were Watching God: A Novel* (New York: J.B. Lippincott Company, 1937), 285, Italics in Original.

Figure 5.2

© Twinsterphoto/Shutterstock.com

Face-to-face, firsthand, from-the-source study is a cornerstone of so much of the interest that so many students bring to the study of political science, and I appreciate the enthusiasm of so many of the students I teach to so eagerly pursue their opportunities to learn outside of the classroom in either internships or work-study opportunities here in the United States, or in study abroad programs overseas that so many of my students take advantage of in their time as students. Firsthand experience is essential for so much of what I do in my own work as a political

Figure 5.3

© Dasha Petrenko/Shutterstock.com

Figure 5.4   Anthony Bourdain

© stock_photo_world/Shutterstock.com

scientist, and I am always grateful to work in an academic field that emphasizes as much as it does the importance of the students I work with exploring firsthand and getting out into the world to see and experience it themselves. I think the benefit of travel is something that is relatively easy for us to explain to students studying political science, so many of whom study comparative and international studies where it is essentially a necessity to get at least some in-person, up-close time. I feel as strongly as anything I do in the research and the work and the writing that I do that this face-to-face, from-the-source studying is one of the most incredible and enriching ways that I know to learn about politics for every part of the discipline of political science.

When political science students think seriously about travel as a part of their studies and their work and their writing as students, I know from years of writing and from fieldwork and travel of my own that there is an incredible body of readings and books we can turn to that tell us and teach us some of the things we can expect in our travels before we set out on our own to do this type of field research. I think of bestselling authors like Barbara Ehrenreich or Evan Wright or others who specialize in this type of face-to-face, firsthand study and writing. I feel any student preparing to travel into the field for their research should read Ehrenreich's 2001 *Nickle and Dimed: On Not Getting by in America* or Wright's *Hella Nation: Looking for Happy Meals in Kandahar, Rocking the Side Pipe, Wingnut's War against the Gap, and Other Adventures with the Totally Lost Tribes of America.*[4] I appreciate too the work political scientists whose careers of fine-grained, firsthand observation of politics help to establish this type of field work in our discipline, names like Richard F. Fenno, Jr. or James C. Scott. I think of Anthony Bourdain and his travels and writing, from his first book, 2000s *Kitchen Confidential: Adventures in the Culinary Underbelly* and 2001s *A Cook's Tour: Global Adventures in Extreme Cuisines*, through his essential later works including 2007s *No Reservations: Around the World on an Empty Stomach.*[5] I think of Barbara W. Tuchman's research on the spot, as she called it, in her visits to the countryside and villages of Belgium, Luxembourg, Northern France, and elsewhere in researching and writing 1962s *The Guns of August* or her travels and visits elsewhere to the places she wrote about in some of her other books.[6] I wrote in Chapter 4 on what I think is the importance of writers leaving their desks and taking the time to take a step away from their computers or their typewriters. I write here in Chapter 5 that I feel writing is always better and easier when writers get up from their desks, get away from their computers or typewriters, and get a chance to talk with others and to think and to, when possible, travel and see firsthand places they write about or that can give them a perspective they bring back to their desks.

I feel one of the most essential parts of travel is that it <u>changes</u> us. I think travel is essential to changing our outlooks and our perspectives that we get only when we visit someplace, but I think it is in changing us when we return that travel's impact is felt for much longer than the time we spend somewhere else. I am almost always a different person when I return from travel somewhere, and I know that most people who travel and visit places for almost any length of time have this same experience. I appreciate that travel is a way of giving me a different perspective when I come back home. Where I live is never the same when I return from my travels, and what I write is almost always <u>better</u> with the experiences I bring back when I travel. I suspect most writers have their own stories of how important some of their travels are to a fresh take on their writing when they return to their desks.[7] I think we never look at where we live

---

4 Barbara Ehrenreich, *Nickel and Dimed: On Not Getting by in America* (New York: Henry Holt and Company, 2001). Evan Wright, *Hella Nation: Looking for Happy Meals in Kandahar, Rocking the Side Pipe, Wingnut's War against the Gap, and Other Adventures with the Totally Lost Tribes of America* (New York: G.P. Putnam's Sons, 2009).

5 Anthony Bourdain, *No Reservations: Around the World on an Empty Stomach* (New York: Bloomsbury, 2007).

6 Barbara W. Tuchman, *Practicing History: Selected Essays by Barbara W. Tuchman* (New York: Alfred A. Knopf, 1981), 20.

7 Stephen King's *On Writing: A Memoir of the Craft* is essential in so many ways for the student just learning to write and for the experienced writer alike, but when I teach King's book, one of the things I like to share with my students is discussion of some of his own travels and his visits that have influenced his writing. I am especially interested in his story he tells elsewhere of a vacation in September 1974 to Colorado's Stanley Hotel at the end of the season when the hotel was closing for the Winter. King's *Secret Windows: Essays and Fiction on the Craft of Writing* tells the story of his trip to Colorado that September and its part in what King calls his "haunted hotel story":

> In late September of 1974, Tabby and I spent a night at a grand old hotel in Estes Park, the Stanley. We were the only guests, as it turned out. The following day, they were going to close the place down for the Winter. Wandering through its corridors, I thought that it seemed to be the perfect—maybe the archetypal—setting for a ghost story. At that time, I had been trying quite hard to write a kidnap novel, this one loosely based on the Patricia Hearst-SLA business, which seemed to have almost every dramatic aspect known to man in it. It is a story that Shakespeare could have hit a mile—that is, if you can imagine Shakespeare somehow couching "fuck all fascist pigs" in iambic pentameter. But the story just wasn't

quite the same after we've seen and lived and experienced life in the places we travel to and visit.

I feel that it is almost always good that when we travel, we are strangers in a strange land. I think it is <u>good</u> that we stand out. I think we <u>should</u> stand out. I think we as visitors, as travelers passing through, do more to respect the people who live there and the places we visit when we stand out. I feel it is respectful to stand out, and I think it is beneficial for those of us wanting to learn, to study, and to work and write about these places to be someone that the people in these places will take the time to show us and will go out of their way to share with us the places they live that we want to learn about and study. I think we want to have people recognize us for who we are, and I feel that most people there will take it upon themselves to show us the places where they live if they sense our curiosity and our interest in their lives and in the places they live.

I know that there is always a time in any visit someplace when you want to blend in, yet I am usually of the opinion that it is better for us as those there to study and to write about someplace to be somewhat obvious and open in our

Figure 5.5

© qoppi/Shutterstock.com

Figure 5.6

© Maria Savenko/Shutterstock.com

intentions to most of those we visit in these places. I sometimes like to tell my students that the challenge of this face-to-face, field research is the challenge of standing out but blending in when we visit and spend time someplace. I feel it is one of the challenges of this kind of face-to-face, field research to be both the outsider who asks questions and who stands out, but also someone who is eager and willing to go with the flow, to go along for the ride and to take the time to take part in whatever is happening there.

---

marching. I went on nuzzling it apathetically for the next few weeks and then decided to put it aside and try what I was thinking of as "the haunted hotel story." I have never written a book that went so smoothly.

"I thought it was time to research in a new setting," King tells us, and his account gives us appreciation for this kind of firsthand research for a novelist like King. Stephen King, *Secret Windows: Essays and Fiction on the Craft of Writing* (New York: Book of the Month Club, 2000), 61–62.

Fenno, Jr.'s 1978 *Home Style: House Members in Their Districts* is exemplary of the face-to-face, find-your-own-way field study in political science, a book that has advice useful to any researcher wanting to travel and to spend time in the places that we study. Fenno is known by many in the field of political science for his "soaking and poking" style of research, and I believe his advice from his work of looking at things firsthand and seeing things as close to the ground as he can get is useful for any student traveling and spending time studying in the field. His is a research of "just hanging around," of "prolonged, unstructured soaking."[8] "Go where you are driven, take what you are given, and when in doubt, be quiet," Fenno, Jr. tells us in the Appendix in 1978s *Home Style*, an addendum that answers many questions of what to expect when doing this kind of research.[9] "[Looking] over the shoulder," "[seeing] through the eyes," "[observing] and [inquiring] into anything and everything," "being nice to people and trying to see the world as they see it," "[being] patient, [coming] on slow, and [feeling] your way along," "[appearing] relaxed," "[blending] into the picture," "[getting] the feel for things," and "[finding] interesting questions emerging in the course of the experience" is all a part of this type of in-the-field research wherever it is done.[10] For students of political science wanting to get out there and to travel and to explore and to see the world, taking the time to look at Fenno, Jr.'s *Home Style* and his other writing is where I would start, whether I was studying here in the United States or traveling overseas to a more distant location.

I think some of the experiences I spent with some of the neighborhood groups organizing on environmental justice issues in Albuquerque, in Los Angeles, in Baton Rouge, in New Orleans, and in other cities and towns across the country in my doctoral dissertation and in its publication in 2000s *Where We Live, Work and Play: The Environmental Justice Movement and the Struggle for a New Environmentalism* as in so many ways similar to what Fenno, Jr.'s Home Style tells us about field research.[11] I read, and reread, *Home Style*'s Appendix with its advice and tips for field research as a part of my preparation for the time I spent on the road and in the field in the places I studied. I took-to-heart Fenno's words of advice for research in the field, and I always kept my schedule as flexible as I could to accommodate the people I met with and spoke with and spent time with everywhere I went in my travels. I fit my schedules to their schedules, I took up every invitation I could to take part in meetings and such with the people I met along the way, and I never turned down an invitation to interview or meet people in their homes if that was better for them. I went to whatever meetings I was invited to, I sat in the back row or out of the way whenever I went to these meetings, and I always took the chance to lend a hand in meetings or even in filing or work around the office if it meant having time to watch these groups at work. I went to protests, and I walked door-to-door with local groups and I sat in the living rooms and stood on the front porches of the homes of the people we visited going door-to-door. I usually did my best to find the closest college or university campus to wherever I was at, and I ended up reading or writing in these campus libraries in between the times that I spent these folks in the field.

---

[8] Richard F. Fenno, Jr., *Home Style: House Members in Their Districts* (New York: Harper Collins Publishers, 1978), 249, 250.
[9] Ibid., 264.
[10] Ibid., xiii, xiv, 251, 252, 263, 264, 291.
[11] Patrick Novotny, *Where We Live, Work and Play: The Environmental Justice Movement and the Struggle for a New Environmentalism* (Westport, CT: Praeger, 2000).

I remember well so many of the conversations and times that I spent with people in these communities in their automobiles, driving either to or from meetings, organizing sessions, or other events to learn more about their work and their communities. I recall several of my best interviews took place on the freeways and the streets in Los Angeles as I drove across the city with organizers whose best times to talk were often in the time they had behind the wheel going to or from community events and meetings. In Louisiana, I remember several middle-of-the-night drives on pitch-black dirt roads in pickup trucks near some of the largest chemical plans along the Mississippi River to see their around-the-clock operations. I sat in the front seats of pickup trucks and had former or current workers at some of those same plants tell me about their operations as well as the impact of some of these operations on their nearby residents and local communities.

I am all too aware that field researchers may not know what is most important to study until they are out there in the field, and I experienced this myself in the time I spent as a part of my doctoral research in Albuquerque, in Los Angeles, in Baton Rouge, in New Orleans, and in other places around the country. I spent what I realized was a far greater amount of time looking at the archives and files of these groups than I ever anticipated before my visits.

Figure 5.7

© GaudiLab/Shutterstock.com

I spent months preparing to do interviews, and I intended to tape-record the bulk of these interviews and type-up transcripts of the tape-recordings.[12] I felt at the time that these transcripts would be the basis of most of my dissertation. I discussed earlier that I decided to take handwritten notes in interviews instead of tape-record interviews almost immediately when I started my field work. I figured I would spent most of my time interviewing, but as it turned out, spending time in offices, attending meetings, and having the chance to look through whatever files they let me look through took on a larger part of my research than I expected before setting foot into the field. I never thought it would prove to be this important, but I spent some of my most productive time looking in filing cabinets and binders of material. I found most had filing-cabinets and closets with stacks of old papers and documents, and I typically found an out-of-the-way place in offices where I could look through whatever material I was given to look at.

I think what I learned more than anything else in my field work for my doctoral dissertation, and in everything I have done since, is that listening is almost always an essential ingredient in the

---

[12] In hindsight, I wish I would had decided to bring a camera on these visits, and to photograph some of the people I met and the places I went to in my dissertation work. I spent so much time preparing for the tape-recording that I ultimately decided not to do that I made no arrangements to have a camera to take photographs on my trips.

work that I do when I am in a face-to-face setting. I take to heart the advice of Fenno, Jr.'s <u>Home</u> <u>Style</u> that talking less ("When in doubt be quiet") and listening more in a friendly, unassuming way is at the heart of successful field work. I think of the story that Robert A. Caro tells us, of writing on his notebooks when taking them with him to his interviews. In large letters on each page of his notebooks, Caro says that he writes the letters "S.U." as a reminder for him to "shut up" when talking with and taking notes while visiting the people he meets with for his interviewing and his research.[13] I admire Caro for this, and I know from his own accounts that he credits his work with the campus paper, *The Daily Princetonian*, at his alma mater, Princeton University, and his stint as a reporter at papers in New Jersey and in New York City after graduation with his in-the-trenches, on-the-ground skills as an interviewer and as a writer.

I know that political science students hoping to prepare for this kind of face-to-face, firsthand, from-the-source field study today can learn a great deal before they take even their first step in their travels from a host of books written on travel by a range of authors. I admire the work of writers like Anthony Bourdain and Rick Steves, and I recommend their writings to my own students and to any political science students taking their first steps into the field. I think that students in political science preparing for their own field research can learn a great deal of what to expect when they are out there from a writer like Anthony Bourdain, whose writings on travel I have recommended to my own students for years. His enthusiasm for music, celebrations, festivals, and especially drinking is an essential part of Bourdain's style in writing on his travels, and he is known for his attention-to-detail in writing about every aspect of the restaurants and gathering places he visits. He is out there and on the road, wherever cooks shop in markets and local stores, wherever wait staff and dishwashers hustle in their crowded kitchens, and wherever bars and taverns stay open late to stay up drinking and sharing his own stories.

In travels that take him to Cambodia, Mexico, Morocco, Portugal, Russia, Vietnam, and elsewhere, Bourdain's 2001 *A Cook's Tour: Global Adventures in Extreme Cuisines* is one of the author's earliest accounts of his travels abroad, of his out-there, roving-about, talking-to-everyday folks travels as he visits shops and finds family-owned restaurants and taverns of all kinds along the way. "[To] cut right to the good stuff, live close to the ground, experience the place from a perspective as close to local as you're going to get," "[to] comb

---

[13] In an April 1990 profile in *Texas Monthly* written by Stephen Harrigan on Caro's field-research and his time spent in Texas in studying the life of President Lyndon Johnson, Caro describes this part of his interviewing and his note-taking:

> "I don't know how good a writer I am," he [Caro] confided as he leafed through a stack of notes that he had transcribed from his sui generis shorthand. (He almost never uses a tape recorder). "But I'm a very good interviewer. I tried to learn how to interview from 2 characters in fiction. One is Inspector Maigret and one is George Smiley. When I was a reporter, I felt I was too aggressive in asking questions. The thing about both of them is that they're quiet and patient. They let the other person talk and really listen to what he's saying. Maigret takes out his pipe and refills it and taps it on the table. Smiley takes his glasses off and wipes them on his necktie. It's a way of keeping themselves quiet. I write 'shut up' in my notebook a lot. Or just 'S.U.' If you looked through my notebooks, you'd see a lot of S.U.'s."

Stephen Harrigan, "The Man Who Never Stops," *Texas Monthly* 18, no. 4 (April 1990): 153.

the world looking for the perfect mix of food and context," and "[to] face extremes of temperature, unusual plumbing arrangements, dodgy food, and the occasional insect on the way to what I was seeking" is his intent, Bourdain tells us in *A Cook's Tour*.[14] Bourdain's travels and his visits with cooks, restaurant owners, market vendors, tour guides, and others in Cambodia and Vietnam are an especially insightful part of *A Cook's Tour*, well-worth reading on their own for anyone thinking of this kind of in-the-field, in-the-mix work.

Figure 5.8

© Azhari Fotolestari/Shutterstock.com

To barhop in the late evening in Basque country bars ("that vaguely defined, famously independent area of southwest France and northern Spain"), to spend mornings at the markets of Saigon, to take a boat ride upriver with a local guide in Cambodia, and so many more go-with-the-flow, throw-caution-to-the-wind moments where he is as comfortable eating at some of the finest restaurants in the places he visits as he is eating at local street vendors along crowded streets make up the essence of Bourdain's *A Cook's Tour*.

"I listen to what people tell me [and] I notice what they eat," Anthony Bourdain tells us in 2006s *The Nasty Bits: Collected Varietal Cuts, Usable Trim, Scraps, and Bones*.

Figure 5.9

© GaudiLab/Shutterstock.com

"[Taking] notice of the details," "[to] be attuned, almost painfully at times, to every nuance around me," "[ending] up too late at night . . . talking shop, talking food," "to eat and drink and drink some more," and "[eating] dinner at midnight" is Bourdain's signature-style in his travel and in his writing in *The Nasty Bits* in story-after-story of his visits with chefs and their restaurants around the world.[15] From New Orleans' Snake and Jake's Christmas Club Lounge to markets and restaurants in Hanoi, Vietnam, Bourdain takes us with him every step of the way from exclusive restaurants to

---

[14] Anthony Bourdain, *A Cook's Tour: Global Adventures in Extreme Cuisines* (New York: Harper Collins Publishers, 2001), 6, 17, 100.

[15] Anthony Bourdain, *The Nasty Bits: Collected Varietal Cuts, Usable Trim, Scraps, and Bones* (New York: Bloomsbury, 2006), xi, 49–50, 64, 79, 139, 143.

Figure 5.10

© Joyseulay/Shutterstock.com

dive bars at 3:00 o'clock in the morning.[16] Travel changes us, Bourdain tells us, and each trip is a reminder always of how much more there is to see and to learn.

I think that political science students should also read some of the work of author Rick Steves, especially his *Travel as a Political Act*, first published by Nation Books in 2009 and in its latest edition from Avalon Travel in 2015. Its latest edition is required-reading for students considering face-to-face research in the field. Filled with photographs taken from

---

[16] Writing from New Orleans, Bourdain tells us of his rules, as he says, for "enjoying yourself in a new and unfamiliar town":

> First rule: Run away from the hotel, as far and as fast as you can. Rule Two: Avoid any place where people like you (meaning out-of-towners or tourists) congregate. Rule Three: When you find a crummy bar clogged with locals who seem to be enjoying themselves, go in, sit down, and start drinking. Be sure to buy a few rounds for your fellow drinkers. At the appropriate moment, inquire of the best places to eat, emphasizing your criteria to go where no tourists have gone before. "Where do *you* eat?" is a good starting point. If you hear the same name twice, take note.

Bourdain, *The Nasty Bits*, 142, Italics in Original.

around the world and with pages of advice and stories of Steves' time abroad, *Travel as a Political Act* is an essential book for students of political science seeking to immerse themselves in their travels and their visits. "Travel a lot, learn about the world, [and] come home with a new perspective," that is in so many words the main argument in *Travel as a Political Act*.[17] "To travel more purposefully," "to learn with an open mind," "to come home and look honestly in the mirror," "to connect with real neighborhoods," "to get out of my comfort zone and simply talk to people," and "[to see] the value of history in understanding our travels, and the value of travel in understanding our history," taken together this is some of the advice offered by Steves.[18] From taking part in demonstrations and political protests in El Salvador to watching tourists overindulge on marijuana in Amsterdam, Steves shares stories of his own travels, including stories (and even some photographs) of his earliest days backpacking as a young man in Europe, where he does most of his traveling and his writing to this day. Steves' *Travel as a Political Act* includes a chapter on the campaign for the legalization of recreational marijuana in the author's home of Washington state and his headline-making involvement in 2012 on the passage of Washington State Initiative 502.

"Knowledge without mileage is bullshit," Henry Rollins, the former lead singer of the punk bank Black Flag and a photographer, poet, and writer of international renown today, tells his audiences. "I am therefore I go" is Rollins' on-the-edge, on-the-move, out-the-door intensity, one that is forever remembered for me in the Rollins who stood just a few feet from me on stage almost thirty years ago when the punk scene exploded with bands like the Dead Kennedys, Black Flag, X, and others.[19] I stood at the edge of the stage at an old skating rink on Delmar Avenue in St. Louis watching Black Flag perform in concert on an August evening in 1985, and I read Rollins' writings today over thirty years later still appreciating the insights in the talks and the writing he does now. I respect and I appreciate Rollins as a performer, photographer, poet, and writer today whose work

---

[17] Rick Steves, *Travel as a Political Act* (Berkeley: Avalon Travel, 2015), 16.

[18] Ibid., ix, 40, 47, 204. I think it is helpful given Steves' thorough and thoughtful approach to travel to discuss the issues of the expenses of traveling and of doing this type of in-the-field study, something that I know from my own personal experience and from my experiences with my students. I certainly think that the digital, on-line sites for airline and other travel options offer the kind of resources for reducing the costs of this type of travel-related research that can make this research possible even for a limited budget. Travel by automobile is one of the more affordable and commonplace ways of doing this kind of in-the-field, travel-related work, and varying the time and schedule of departure might impact the expense of this kind of travel.

[19] "I read all the books I can but I know that there's nothing in any of those books that can teach me what I really need to know," Rollins writes in 2009's *A Preferred Blur: Reflections, Inspections, and Travel in All Directions 2007*. "I need experience." 2009s *A Preferred Blur* takes the reader along with some of Rollins' travels to Dubai, Iran, Israel, Jordan, and elsewhere, and includes his knowledge-without-mileage idea:

> The equation I have been using for many years means more and more to me as time goes on: knowledge without mileage equals bullshit. That's been the thing that gets me out the door more often than not. I can read all the books and do all the thinking I want but without getting out into it, what good is anything I know? I am therefore I go. That's it

Henry Rollins, A Preferred Blur: Reflections, Inspections, and Travel in All Directions 2007 2.13.61, 2009, 22.

Figure 5.11

© Mat Hayward/Shutterstock.com

is a fascinating catalogue of travel photography, spoken-word performances, and writings on his visits to some of the most desolate corners of the world.

Henry Rollins' 2011 *Occupants: Photographs and Writings by Henry Rollins* is a book that tells a story from the first thing we see in its front-cover photograph taken by Rollins of a Democratic People's Republic of Korea (DPRK) soldier in the Demilitarized Zone (DMZ) to its back-cover of photograph of a teacher in her classroom in Southern Sudan, and in every photograph and every page of writing in between. In *Occupants*, Rollins tells us of his travels to some of the most conflict-stricken places in the world. "I travel as far and as wide as I can to try and learn as much as possible along the way," Rollins tells us in the introduction of *Occupants*. "I think the more one sees, the better," he says. "The journeys I have made have humbled me greatly."[20] "To know more and see more," "[to] work at trying to understand as best I can," "[to] see what I see and meet whom I meet," "[to] take the first opportunity to leap into the greatest environment of uncertainty," "to really get an understanding of what has happened," "to go there and see what I could," and "full immersion" is

---

[20] Henry Rollins, *Occupants: Photographs and Writings by Henry Rollins* (Chicago: Chicago Review Press, 2010), xi.

everything for Rollins.[21] "It's just me, a camera, and a notebook," Rollins tells us, and his photographs and writings from his travels tell the story of the struggles for survival in some of the most conflict-stricken parts of the globe, including Afghanistan, Iran, Iraq, Mali, Syria, South Africa, Sri Lanka, and Vietnam. "No book is going to teach you," Rollins tells us toward the end of *Occupants*. "If you really want to know, you really have to go," Rollins advises.[22] I am not sure that I know any other book that makes this argument as clearly and intensely as Rollins' *Occupants*, and I would regard it as must-reading for any student of political science or anyone taking that first step out into the world.

I think anyone wanting to take the first steps to doing this firsthand-style studying in the field should spend some time reading writings by figures like Anthony Bourdain or Rick Steves or Henry Rollins, but I also believe that at a certain point, there is only so much one can learn about this type of research from reading even these books, and that there comes a time when we need to take the first steps and set out and get out there and figure it out ourselves, knowing that there is a learning curve in this type of research, that we will make our share of mistakes along the way, that it will get easier the more we travel and take the time to learn and get to know people we meet along the way. I feel it is important for students of political science to take the time to figure out this firsthand type of studying for themselves, and I think this means accepting that each of us will make mistakes along the way, and that there'll be moments along the way when we'll want to turn back more than once along the way.

Figure 5.12

© J. Kelavicius/Shutterstock.com

I think it is important for us to get out of the door and on the sidewalk as much as possible in the places we visit, and I feel it is important to walk as much as you can whenever you are there. I feel it is always helpful to walk whenever we can. I especially like to walk early in the mornings to watch cities or

---

[21] Ibid., xi, 62, 118, 132. Reading, as I discussed in Chapter 2, is an activity that easily is shared with and talked about with people around us, and writing, as I discussed in Chapter 3, is also something social in our sharing of our work and our writing with others. In this instance, though, Rollins' discussion certainly raises the idea that the field research and travels of this type is sometimes something done, for a variety of reasons, by a person alone. I think Rollins references to this in 2010s *Occupants* is a useful discussion of this.

[22] Rollins, *Occupants*, 119. In his writings from his 2010 travels in Mali, Rollins offers some thoughts that put a great deal of this into perspective:

> Sometimes you see things that are so amazing, so humbling, that you realize you will always be a student, that you will never know enough, that you will never have enough hours in the day or years in your life to get more than a rudimentary understanding of the world and how it really is. The best you can do is approximate, sidestep your expectations and all that you project on to them, and let it be. You will never be more alive than in those rare moments.

Rollins, *Occupants*, 142.

towns begin to stir at the start of their day. I like to walk early in the morning whenever I can when I visit someplace for the first time to get the feel for the place. I mentioned in Chapter 2 that one of the places I like to most often visit when I travel are bookstores, and I especially like to find small, independent bookstores and used bookstores. I like to find local newsstands whenever I can, and I like to stay as close to a downtown area as possible whenever I stay somewhere. I purchase whatever daily papers I can when I visit for as long I am there, and I carry them with me as I make the way out into the day, giving me something to look at other than checking messages on my phone for the inevitable standing-in-lines of visits to historical locations or points of interest when traveling.

I <u>read</u> when I travel. I enjoy reading when I travel in some ways as much or more than I enjoy it when I am working back in my office or at home, as I mentioned in Chapter 2. Whether I am returning somewhere I have visited before or traveling somewhere to visit for the first time, I typically travel almost in the way that I might approach a work of scholarly research. I enjoy reading up on the places that I travel and visit in the weeks <u>before</u> I travel there, and

I enjoy reading <u>while</u> I travel, as I wrote in Chapter 2. I scan my own digitally archived files for stories, and I look up stories on LexisNexis Academic and elsewhere.

I like to visit bookstores when I arrive to the destinations in my travels, and I find looking at bookstores in the places I visit to be one of the best ways to connect with the culture and history in these places. I do not read tour guides or travel-related books in a traditional sense, but I instead like to read histories or even novels or short stories on these places whenever I can as well as to read whatever newspapers I can find that give me the wide-angle view of the

Figure 5.13

© Hardian/Shutterstock.com

places I am staying in my travels. I read <u>before</u> I travel someplace, and I continue reading while I am <u>there</u>, and I still read keep reading about these places when I <u>return home</u>, often spurring interest in returning later with even more insight and knowledge of the local history and landscape.

I write when I travel. I take plenty of legal pads and pens with me whenever I travel, and I send e-mails with materials and notes on things that I read and study as I travel. I know travel teaches me things about places that I never would learn without being there, and I know for a fact that it improves my writing with new ideas and thoughts that I can sometimes begin writing while I am still away from my desk. I usually bring a laptop computer for longer trips, and I especially like the portability of Google Docs to jot down notes and to write as I travel. I tapped out many of the first ideas for this book on my phone using Google Docs over the span of several months, including travels that took me away from my home for about three weeks in that time. I started this book by opening several different Google Docs files for each chapter but then decided it was easier to work on the preliminary notes and thoughts for this book in a single Google Docs file that I found to be much easier to scroll through and write on my phone instead of opening and closing different Google Docs files whenever I thought about a topic. Every thought, even the smallest ideas I typed in the Google Docs file for this book if I felt it was in any way helpful, and I did much of this while traveling, sitting in airports, visiting several cities including Washington, DC. I even worked on the Google Docs file during what might have been a frustrating three-hour cab ride courtesy of an airline that overbooked a flight I was supposed to be on in this time. I spent most of that three hours in the cab with my phone in hand tapping away my notes in Google Docs for this book.

I say all of this because I think writing while we travel and while we are in the field for our research is some of the most important writing we do in our work. I think that most field researchers with any experience will tell you that time in the field is not simply time spent conducting interviews, gathering material, and taking notes on everything we see happening, it also is a time to think through and even begin to do some writing from these materials. I think if anything is different today from the time when I did my first field research in Albuquerque, in Baton Rouge, in New Orleans, and in other places around the country, it is

Figure 5.14

© MBR9292/Shutterstock.com

our ability to write on laptop computers, tablets, or phones in the field. Thanks to Google Docs and to e-mail that lets me send notes to myself that I can easily printout and read when I return to my desk, I can write in the field and not just gather materials. I feel that there is sometimes no better way than to study away from the office and away from the desk, and I know I sometimes blur my reading, my writing, and my interest in the historical perspective together in my travels wherever they take me. I enjoy my travels and I certainly spend time taking in lots of things when I travel for enjoyment that in no way relate to anything that I research, but I make the most of traveling whether it is airplane flights, standing in line at a museum or riding on a subway, or simply those quiet, unexpected moments where I can sometimes do some of my most enjoyable reading and writing.

Clichés of getting outside of one's comfort zone when we travel are often just that, yet just as often, the truth is that travel is something that lets us meet people in some of the most unexpected ways and to learn things one would never learn in the library or in the office or the classroom. I know well that is the same for the in-the-field, in-person, up-close research that is essential to so much of the field research in the study of political science today. Face-to-face, field study is a way of taking us to the places <u>where</u> people live and of studying the <u>way</u> that people live. Where, as I said in Chapter 1, is an essential part of the study of politics, and this is how we study where by getting out and taking to the road and going there.

I like the sense of adventure in traveling and field research, even if it means spending a day's drive to look through archives or microfilmed materials in a library. I did this with some of the research in 2007s *This Georgia Rising: Education, Civil Rights, and the Politics of Change in Georgia in the 1940s*, driving halfway across Georgia in daylong road trips to archives from the Richard B. Russell Library for Political Research and Studies at the University of Georgia to local libraries in Macon and elsewhere for even just a few hours to look at microfilm records or folders of materials.[23] I enjoyed having the chance to get away from my desk and out of the office for a few hours, and I liked having the chance to clear my head and come to back at the end of the day or that next morning if I stayed overnight with a few more footnotes and sometimes some stories to share. I remember these trips well for letting me see some of the towns in Georgia where some of the history I wrote about in *This Georgia Rising* was made, of talking with archivists, librarians, and other researchers working in the stacks and with microfilm machines, of walking downtown for a few hours for lunch or a cup of coffee before heading back home and back to the office where I returned to my reading and to my students and to my teaching and to my writing. I think <u>that</u> is the real value of traveling and of field research and spending time away from our desks and away from our classrooms and our libraries, learning the <u>feel</u> of a place where we visit and the feeling we get when we take the time to walk, to wander, and to learn and see what no reel of microfilm or footnote in a book can ever tell us.

---

[23] Patrick Novotny, *This Georgia Rising: Education, Civil Rights, and the Politics of Change in Georgia in the 1940s* (Macon: Mercer University Press, 2007).

CHAPTER
6

All Political Science Is Local

"The 'what' of Harold D. Lasswell's famous definition of politics is a complex universe in itself," the late Murray Edelman tells us in one of his most important books, 1964s *The Symbolic Uses of Politics*.[1] I remember well Edelman's seminars at the University of Wisconsin-Madison. I studied with him in my first year as a doctoral student at Wisconsin, in the last year Edelman taught before his retirement. I sat in the seminar room on the fourth floor of North Hall at Wisconsin as Edelman turned the pages in his folders of notes and spoke to his students seated around the seminar table, and I remember most of all his passion for casting as wide of an intellectual perspective as possible when talking with us about the study of political science, encouraging us as students in his seminars to draw from critical theory, feminist theory, Marxism, and whatever other intellectual perspectives the work of our dissertations required. I recall as clearly as anything Murray's insistence to his students that we needed always to understand the importance of values in the study of politics.

I remember like it was yesterday sitting in Edelman's seminars in that room on the fourth floor of North Hall as he insisted over and over to us that we as political scientists needed to study values, to appreciate the filters and the forces that shape the way that politics is perceived, portrayed, and symbolically expressed. He had just published his *Constructing the Political Spectacle* when I had the chance to study with him in his last year of teaching, and he was writing then what I still feel is one of his most important books, 1995s *From Art to Politics: How Artistic Creations Shape Political Conceptions*.[2] It was Edelman's life's work to push his fellow political scientists to study culture, to

---

[1] Murray Edelman, *The Symbolic Uses of Politics* (Urbana: The University of Illinois Press, 1964), 43. Edelman's discussion of Lasswell's work as quoted here in the opening chapter of 1964s *The Symbolic Uses of Politics*, appeared for the first time in his October 1960 article, "Symbols and Political Quiescence," in *The American Political Science Review*. Murray Edelman, "Symbols and Political Quiescence," *The American Political Science Review* 54, no. 3 (October 1960): 794.

[2] His *Constructing the Political Spectacle* had been published shortly before I arrived at the University of Wisconsin-Madison, and I knew Murray's work and was eager to study with him even before I arrived on campus but his retirement that year marked the end of his teaching. I regard it to this day as one of the greatest opportunities in my career to have had the chance to study with him in the last year of his teaching in the Political Science Department, and it was in that time that he was finishing *From Art to Politics*. 1995s *From Art to Politics* is one of my favorite books of Edelman's career, and I enjoyed working on several projects related to art and politics in the time we worked together and after, including a paper that I completed that gained some interest from several faculty members

Figure 6.1 North Hall, University of Wisconsin-Madison

© EQRoy/Shutterstock.com

study language, and to study symbols and the expressive and perceptive filters of politics. I learned some of the most important lessons of my work as a political scientist in those seminars in North Hall with Edelman, and I did my best in the years after his retirement to hold true to his teaching the importance of art and culture and language and symbols in the study of political science.

I started this book on the opening pages of Chapter 1 discussing the work of Lasswell as well, and I made the case that political scientists wanting to take their perspective from 1936s *Politics: Who Gets What, When, How* need to think, as Edelman did so well, not just about, as Edelman asked, <u>what is the what</u> in Lasswell's famous formulation, but think too about what is <u>left out</u> by Lasswell. Why, where, and who has gotten what before, as I said at the beginning of Chapter 1, are, I believe, all a part of thinking through politics in the widest sense.[3] I think political scientists need

---

across the Wisconsin campus on the National Museum of American Art's 1991 "The West as America: Reinterpreting Images of the Frontier, 1820–1920." I credit Murray for my continuing interest, almost twenty-five years later, on art and the works of artists as impacted by and impactful on politics.

[3] The late Clifford Geertz—known for his life's work in the study of culture, of his years living abroad in Indonesia and Morocco that formed the basis for several of his books including 1968s *Islam Observed: Religious Development in Morocco and Indonesia*, of his calls for to a detail-focused, fact-heavy form of writing of the places he studied known

to be mindful of motivations, we need to take care to keep the historical perspective in mind, and we're always better off when it is possible for us to go in person ourselves to visit the places we write about. When we think with the kind of historical perspective that I discussed in Chapter 4 and when we get out of the classroom to travel and to get to know people in the places where they live, as I discussed in Chapter 5, I believe we can better understand why, where, and what has been gotten <u>before</u>.

"'Let me tell you something I learned years ago,' he said," the late Speaker of the House Tip O'Neill tells us of his father's advice shortly after O'Neill lost the first campaign in his career in his bid for a seat on the Cambridge City Council. "All politics is local," O'Neill tells of his father's advice shared with his son in the mostly Irish, working-class wards in North Cambridge, Massachusetts, words that O'Neill took to heart in his career and took with him to Washington, DC, in his 1952 election as the Representative for Massachusetts' 8th Congressional District, held by John F. Kennedy until his bid that same year for the Senate, and as the forty-seventh Speaker of the United States House of Representatives.[4] I take O'Neill's advice from his father to heart as well, and I think the words both O'Neill and his father knew well and lived in those North Cambridge wards is an essential perspective that is all too often left out of too much of the work in political science.

I feel it's important here in the closing pages of this book to make the case for students of political science to <u>connect</u> with the people around us and with the places that we call home. I think it is

Figure 6.2

as thick description, of his famous interpretations of the expressive differences between "winks" and "blinks," of his immersive involvement in the places he studied including he and his wife's being swept up in a fleeing crowd from an illegal Balinese cockfight, published for the first time in Winter 1972s *Daedalus* in his "Deep Play: Notes on the Balinese Cockfight," and his interdisciplinary, path-breaking studies of history, ideology, and the symbols of culture—studied the dynamics of politics, specifically Harold D. Lasswell's famous formulation:

> Thrones may be out of fashion, and pageantry too, but political authority still requires a cultural frame in which to define itself and advance its claim, and so does opposition to it . . . . The enfoldment of political life in general conceptions of how reality is put together did not disappear with dynastic continuity and divine right. Who gets What, When, Where, and How is as culturally distinctive a view of what politics is, and in its own way as transcendental, as defense of "wisdom and rightwiseness," the celebration of "The Daymaker's Equal," or the capricious flow of *baraka*.

Clifford Geertz, *Local Knowledge: Further Essays in Interpretive Anthropology* (New York: Basic Books, 1983), 143–144.

[4] Tip O'Neill, *Man of the House: The Life and Political Memoirs of Speaker Tip O'Neill* (New York: Random House, 1987), 26.

important for political scientists to do their best whenever possible to connect the research they do and the writing they do with the communities and the places where they live. I think one of the simplest and easiest ways political scientists can do this is to write in simple, easy-to-understand language whenever possible, even when writing on the seemingly more esoteric and presumably difficult-to-explain ideas.

I think one of the best starting points for political scientists when we want to connect with our communities and with the people around us, be they our friends, family, or students, is to do our best when writing to write in simple terms about the lived realities, the shared realities of politics. I think it is easier to do so when we are more closely tied to our communities and to our family and friends whose perspectives and thoughts on politics we can take into consideration and listen to as we write about the topics we write on in our work as political scientists. I believe that the more closely we are tied to the friends and people around us in the places we live, the better we are as political scientists in making our work meaningful and relevant to a wider audience.

I have said in Chapter 1 and again here in Chapter 6 that some of the most important questions that political scientists need to come to terms with and to think through are those having to do with why, that is, those questions involving motivations and values that help to filter and to foster different actions and what not. When we study why, we delve into motivations and reasoning and values, all of which I feel are always going to be understood better the closer we can get and the more we can listen, look carefully, and see for ourselves, up-close, in-person.

How are we possibly ever going to understand why if we are not in the habit of asking people about their motivations and their reasoning? How can we ever know why unless we talk with them about the reasons they feel and think and act the way that they do? If we don't listen to people talk with us and tell us why they think the way they do and why they do the things they do, how can we ever really understand or know what is going on? I am a big believer in the idea that face-to-face involvement in whatever we study grounds us, it keeps us focused. I feel strongly that it keeps us from getting too lost in theory or models or abstractions as political scientists, and I think it takes us closer to the empathy and the understanding that I wrote about in Chapter 1 in my discussion of Woodrow Wilson's plea for his fellow political scientists to appreciate the "intensely human" aspects in everything we study as political scientists.

Figure 6.3

© Sheila Fitzgerald/Shutterstock.com

I do think that it is important for us to be able to talk and to teach and to write as political scientists in a straightforward way about whatever specific subjects we study. I am always better off in the research and the writing I do when I use <u>clear</u> examples, when I do my best to write straightforward explanations, and when I write as descriptively as I can. I said in Chapter 3 that I feel the writer is responsible for is doing what I like to say is the reader's work for them. I feel as a writer I owe it to my readers to do everything I can to write in a clear, simple, well-organized way, and I leave a well-marked trail of breadcrumbs, if you will, in my footnotes and references to help my readers find the material and sourcing I use in my evidence and examples. I want to do everything I can to anticipate any confusion or questions on the part of my reader, and I want to take any uncertainty a reader might have into consideration in every sentence I write, every footnote I add, and every sentence or paragraph that I write and rewrite to make sure I am getting it right.

I think the way that we connect with our community and with the people around us and with the places that we live and call home is an essential part of being a political scientist. I think one of the parts of Chapters 2 and 3 that I take to heart in everything that I do is talking about the reading and the writing I do with family and with friends and students while I am working on it. In Chapters 2 and 3, I talked about the importance of talking, and I hope with the reader's indulgence and at the risk of repeating myself that I might say a few more words on this here in the closing of my book. I said in the closing words at the end of Chapter 3, and I say here again in Chapter 6, that I don't want to necessarily belabor these conversations with too much detail or <u>bore</u> the people that matter the most to me around me by droning on about the writing that I do. I do, though, like to share sometimes something as simple as just a few words with my friends and with the people who I am around every day about the latest work that I am writing, even if it's nothing more than just letting folks know whether it's going well and the words are flowing or that I've hit a wall or slowed down for whatever reason in my writing.

Figure 6.4

© Shutterstock.com

I find that even the most casual comments or asides from my family or friends or the folks I see every day to ask about my writing or to lend a sympathetic ear for a few minutes is something that can lift my mood and keep me on track in what I am doing when I write. I think the simple fact of the people who mean the most to us and who are closest to us knowing that we are writing and that when they see us, they know enough of what we are doing in it to ask us how our writing is going, I think this is something that is sometimes underappreciated by some writers.

I take exception to any writer who might say that they won't bother talking about their writing since it would take too much time to explain it or that their family or friends would find it boring or uninteresting. Quite to the contrary, I find that most of the people I am closest to and who I see the most often take an interest whenever I am writing something at the time, and I take a great deal of satisfaction to have them ask about what I am writing and to let me talk for a few minutes about whatever I am working on at the time before we talk about something else.

I find that most people are genuinely curious and interested to know what it is that I am writing, and I find most people to be gracious when it comes to giving me a few minutes to talk about what I am working on with them. I might try out some ideas with them that may or may not end up in the writing that I am doing, and I sometimes find myself either talking myself into or out of writing about something when I talk with people and try it out by talking about it with them. I think we as writers can sometimes fail to fully appreciate and understand just how important the people we are around every day are to the writing that we do, and I think talking about our work and our writing with our friends, family, or others is especially helpful as we try to finish up writing something we are working on.

I know I am always better off when I can step away from my desk and push off my writing for an afternoon or even a few days, and I know that the only way I am able to do this is by telling my family and friends and folks around me that I am writing but also by letting them know that I am not so wrapped up in my writing that I can't return a text message or talk for a few minutes or even put my writing aside to get away from the desk for a drink or a swim or a walk. To paraphrase the character Joe MacMillan, played by actor Lee Pace, in AMC's drama television series Halt and Catch Fire on early days of the personal computer industry, writing isn't the thing. It's the thing that gets us to the thing.

I titled this chapter "All Political Science is Local" in my long admiration and appreciation for the insights of the late Speaker of the House O'Neill's words of advice, and I did so because much like writing, I think everything that we do as political scientists is improved when we connect it with the places we call home and when we talk with and listen to the people closest to us who are around us all the time and who mean the most to us. When I say all political science is local, I really should say that all political science research is local. It is in our involvement in our communities. It is in our connections with the places we live. It is in our reading local newspapers, and it is in our listening to conversations and discussions of all kinds. It is in a friend or family member putting something into words that send us scrambling for a piece of paper and a pen to jot down a note either on what they said, or something said that triggered something in our thinking. I truly appreciate and I am grateful for the incredible opportunities that I have as a writer, and I feel that talking with and especially listening to the people closest to me that matter the most to me is something that I hope makes me a better, more conscientious writer.

I like to think I am a better writer because I am a part of my community, and I take part in things locally where I live that let me widen my perspectives and thinking on some of the topics that I am interested in. I see this in almost every part of my work with our county's Historical Society and with other activities and events I take part in throughout our community, and I like to think that some part of this is my eagerness to listen and to pay close attention to these types of lectures, presentations, programs, and other events. I am a Board Member of the Historical Society in my county, and I enjoy every conversation with the members of our organization and every lecture and presentation we host for giving me some new story or something new about the history of a community I have called home for more than twenty years.

I am incredibly fortunate to have a chance almost daily to experience the words of President Harry Truman that I selected for the title of Chapter 4, "there is nothing new in the world except the history you do not know."[5] I like to learn something <u>new</u> about history almost every day, and I learn this history because I pay attention, I listen and I read whatever I can get my hands on, and I use my Google News Alerts and other e-mail and social media like Twitter to keep up with the work and writing of some of my favorite historians along with the Smithsonian Institution's National Museum of African-American History and Culture (NMAAHC), the National Museum of American History (NMAH), the Rock and Roll Hall of Fame and Museum in Cleveland, the National Portrait Gallery (NPG), and others.

Figure 6.5   The Newseum, Washington, D.C.

© Richard Cavalleri/Shutterstock.com

---

[5] William Hillman, *Mr. President: The First Publication from the Personal Diaries, Private Letters, Papers, and Revealing Interviews of Harry S. Truman, President of the United States of America* (New York: Farrar Straus and Young, 1952), 81.

I feel I am incredibly fortunate to have learned so much of the local history where I live, and I love to listen to the stories I am told by the people I know through the county's Historical Society and other groups and organizations I am involved in. I think writing as a political scientist with an interest in a historical perspective, I have grown much more attuned to listening to the stories told by the people who have lived their whole lives in a place I have only lived for the past twenty years or so. I can think of at least two or three of my publications that I wrote because of my interest and listening to the stories told by folks in our community. I wrote 2007s *This Georgia Rising: Education, Civil Rights, and the Politics of Change in Georgia in the 1940s* because of the interest that several longtime university administrators, archivists, and librarians on my campus had in telling me the history of Georgia Southern University and several of its Presidents in particular, Dr. Guy Wells and Dr. Marvin Pittman.[6] I had the incredible good fortune shortly after my arrival at Georgia Southern University to meet several administrators as well as library archivists on the campus who took the time to tell me the stories of the educational leadership and later the political attacks on Presidents Wells and Pittman by one of Georgia's most infamous Governors, Eugene Talmadge. I listened to these stories, I looked up old archived, microfilmed newspapers from the 1930s and 1940s, and I talked with people from our community for several years before deciding to begin writing on the legacy of leadership of Wells and Pittman, writing that soon widened its historical perspective to the entire decade of the 1940s when most of these changes and controversies took place in Georgia's state higher education system.

I wrote another work that I am especially proud of because of some of the same history I learned and some of the stories I was told by people I met in my travels around the state of Georgia in the research and the work that I did in writing *This Georgia Rising*. As I talked with people in my own community and as I traveled around the state to visit local libraries and work with their local archives when materials couldn't be loaned out, I read and learned much more than I might have ever imagined at the time about another major transformation during Georgia's wartime decade of the 1940s, specifically the arrival of commercial broadcast television in Atlanta and its growth across the state to cities like Augusta, Columbus, Macon, and elsewhere.

I learned early in my work with microfilm newspapers with this project to look at the entire page of the newspaper, something that I discussed in Chapter 4. I leaned forward in my chair sometimes squinting at the pages of microfilmed papers as they spooled through the microfilm reader, and I kept my eyes out for not just news items of the higher education controversies and elections in Georgia in the 1940s, but also I looked for any possible other news items or stories that might turn into another project, and I gathered a large enough amount of these news items on commercial television's arrival in Georgia beginning in September 1948 with Atlanta's WSB-TV to write an article on this for the Georgia Historical Society's *The Georgia Historical Quarterly*.[7] I think that writing this article in *The Georgia Historical Quarterly* on Georgia's television history in the 1940s helped keep my interest strong such that I researched the decade of the 1940s for

---

[6] Patrick Novotny, *This Georgia Rising: Education, Civil Rights, and the Politics of Change in Georgia in the 1940s* (Macon GA: Mercer University Press, 2007).

[7] Patrick Novotny, "The Impact of Television on Georgia, 1948–1952," *The Georgia Historical Quarterly* 91, no. 3 (Fall 2007): 324–347.

Figure 6.6 Forsyth Park, Savannah, Georgia

© Lawrence Roberg/Shutterstock.com

commercial television with perhaps a great deal more interest than I would have otherwise in writing Chapter 6 of my 2014 book, *The Press in American Politics, 1787–2012*.

I shared in Chapter 3 the words I like to share with my students of the French scientist Louis Pasteur, who said, "*Dans les champs de l'observation, le hasard ne favorise que les esprits préparés*," or in a rough translation, "chance only favors the mind which is prepared."[8] I share these words with my students when I teach research and writing for political science majors because I want them to appreciate and understand that every conversation, every book they read, every lecture they hear, everything they do has the potential to spark an idea or a thought they can use in their own work and their own writing. The more conversations they have, the more closely they listen, the more they read and think and talk about what it is they are interested with the people around them, the more likely it is that they will have

---

[8] Rene Vallery-Radot, *The Life of Pasteur*, trans. R. L. Devonshire (New York: Doubleday, Page and Company, 1923), 76.

those moments of clarity and insight that will set them on their way in their own work. I tell my students the story of my work on my article on Georgia's commercial television history in the 1940s as an example of this that I myself experienced, having in no way intended to write on this part of Georgia's history yet listening and reading and writing notes while I worked on another project that left me prepared and with enough material to come back to write my essay for *The Georgia Historical Quarterly* after completing *This Georgia Rising*.

I think, too, in this regard of another writing project that I almost came upon quite by accident in some sense, and that I essentially became interested in not only through my interest in the local history of the community I call home, but also through my conversations with people who have lived their whole lives here and who took the time to talk with me and tell me some of the histories of local changes and controversies over the years. Shortly after I arrived in the community I've called home for some twenty years now, I was told by some of my faculty colleagues who had lived and taught here for some time of a Supreme Court case

Figure 6.7

© Lindasj22/Shutterstock.com

involving a local lumber company that had gone out of business back in the 1970s. I started to learn a lot and to take in a lot of the local history and stories of our community upon my arrival, and I also spent a significant amount of time in Savannah at the time whose history I also absorbed with a kind of wide-eyed wonder, but I always in my mind came back to that story of a former lumber company in my newly adopted hometown that had been a part of a case heard before the Supreme Court of the United States. Not every town boasts such a chapter in their history, and I decided that once I had the time, I would devote some time to learning more and perhaps even writing about this history.

In the meantime, I met even more of the folks in our community as I settled in and set down roots, so to speak, and I learned more about the history of the lumber company and even met some of the family of the company's founder, the late Fred W. Darby. Eventually, with the encouragement and support of some local folks, including members of the county Historical Society, I wrote up one of the first accounts ever written of the local history of this story and of the Supreme Court case, 1941s <u>United States v. Darby Lumber Company</u>.[9] I was honored to assist in the placement of a roadside historical marker by the county Historical Society at the edge of the company's property, now a mostly overgrown field with no remaining structures or visible reminders of the once-thriving lumber company that closed its doors in the early 1970s, and I feel still incredibly humbled to have been a part of telling the local story of this Supreme Court case in a way that I hope can now be told and retold for years to come.

I think it <u>matters</u> in the work we do as political scientists to be a <u>part</u> of the places we live, and I think the more we do to take an interest in our communities and the more we connect with the people with whom we live in these places, the more likely we are as political scientists to be more grounded in our work and in our writing. The phrase "think globally, act locally" is one of those clichés that we seem to see everywhere all the time but in this case, I think it is useful in the way I think about political science as needing to connect our study of politics in the places we live whenever it is appropriate to the subject. Realistically, of course, I know that not all political scientists will be able to relate their work to, say, a small South Georgia college town, but there are ways still to do our research that can connect it with the places we live, whether it is being a part of, say, library talks by authors (or even by making sure that libraries where we live have copies of the books we write and maybe even contact information like an e-mail address for our local readers might want to contact us to learn more about our work) or speaking as visiting lecturers in classes or to local groups. I think even the simple habit of, say, reading the local newspaper, of following issues in our communities as they are debated on social media, of attending debates of candidates for local office, or even just meeting our colleagues or students in locations like bakeries or coffee shops out in the community for conversations is sometimes a way for us to connect with and to be a part of the places we live.

"Let us note simply that, in defiance of the most solemn dictates of the democratic ideology, Americans lose rather than gain interest steadily as their electoral obligations move closer to

---

[9] Patrick Novotny, "United States v. Darby Lumber Company, Statesboro, Georgia, 1939–1941," *Statesboro Magazine* 6, no. 2 (March 2005): 56–61.

home," Clinton Rossiter tells us in 1960s *Parties and Politics in America*. "Elections to those offices that are closest to home, where the issues are immediate and the candidates known, generally attract only a tiny percentage of the voting population."[10] I regard Rossiter's *Parties and Politics in America* as one of the great books in the study of the history of American political parties, and his insight for "those offices that are closest to home" in his 1960 book is something I, too, am mindful of as a political scientist. In a day when by some accounts only one-third of Americans can correctly identify the name of the Mayor, when attendance at City Council meetings hovers at precipitously low levels in some places, and when the circulation and subscription of local newspapers is plummeting in the era of on-line digital media, I don't believe it is sufficient for us to say as political scientists that it is the responsibility of, say, only those who study American institutions or who study state and local government.

I think all of us in the field of political science all have a responsibility to be a part of this conversation, and to be a part of connecting with the places we live. Whatever else it is that I think we need to do as political scientists—asking why, where, and who has gotten what before, reading widely, writing clearly, getting out of our offices and out of the classroom, widening our view of politics to take in a historical perspective—I think it matters more than all of this for us as political scientists to be part of the places we live, and I think it begins for us as political scientists who want to make a difference by making the time and taking the time to take on, in the words of President Barack Obama, "the same proud title, the most important office," in our communities and in our country: citizen.

---

[10] Clinton Rossiter, *Parties and Politics in America* (New York: Cornell University Press, 1960), 30.

CPSIA information can be obtained
at www.ICGtesting.com
Printed in the USA
LVHW01s1212141217
559490LV00002B/4/P

9 781524 951436